P9-ASK-689

Legal Almanac Series No. 24

THE ELECTION PROCESS: VOTING LAWS AND PROCEDURES

by Alan Reitman , LL.B.
Associate Executive Director,
American Civil Liberties Union

and Robert B. Davidson, J.D.
Harlan Fiske Stone Scholar,
Columbia University

1972 OCEANA PUBLICATIONS, INC.
Dobbs Ferry, New York

CARNEGIE LIBRARY
LIVINGSTONE COLLEGE
SALISBURY, N. C. 28144

This is the twenty-fourth number in a series of LEGAL ALMANACS which bring you the law on various subjects in nontechnical language. These books do not take the place of your attorney's advice, but they can introduce you to your legal rights and responsibilities. This volume replaces the former edition of Legal Almanac No. 24, Voting and Election Laws - Laws for Voters, by Constance E. Smith.

© Copyright 1972 by Oceana Publications, Inc.

Library of Congress Cataloging in Publication Data

Reitman, Alan.
    The election process--voting laws and procedures.

    (Legal almanac series, no. 24)
    "This volume replaces ... Voting and election laws--
laws for voters, by Constance E. Smith."
    1.   Election law--United States--States.   I.   Davidson,
Robert B., joint author.   II.   Title.
KF4886.Z95R4   342'.73'07   70-104115
ISBN 0-379-11069-5

Manufactured in the United States of America

342.73
R379

TABLE OF CONTENTS

85244

TABLE OF CHARTS

APPENDICES

ACKNOWLEDGMENTS

No book is written without the assistance of many people, who either directly or indirectly are involved with the work. This book, a complete revision of an earlier publication by Dr. Constance E. Smith plus much additional material, is no exception.

I am grateful to my friends and colleagues in the American Civil Liberties Union, who, while not consulted on this book, helped to shape my thinking over the years about the value, content and meaning of personal expression, voting rights and the democratic process. I especially appreciate the suggestions and steady interest of Aryeh Neier, executive director of the ACLU.

I am profoundly grateful to my wife, Miriam, and my daughter, Janet, for their patience, understanding and encouragement. Their good cheer, while sharing with me many difficult moments during preparation of the manuscript, was a source of comfort and strength. Thanks are due Sidney and Marion Reitman for their friendly inquiries into the progress of the publication, and their "hideaway" basement office, where the book primarily was written. I also want to note the good help of Cris MacDonald and Timothy Tyson in the typing of the manuscript.

A number of other people and organizations provided valuable information and research leads, and they are properly credited in the Researcher's Acknowledgements below.

A final word, not of acknowledgement but of caution and advice to readers. This is primarily a reference book for use by those interested in the electoral process, and is based on facts and information gathered from diverse sources. All the information has been updated to the greatest extent possible through March, 1972. But special attention should be drawn to the fact that state legislatures are constantly changing state election codes. These revisions of election laws make it all the more necessary that the voter verify the specific information reported in this book with local election officials. The reader is also urged to find out how the voting law is applied, as some registrars and other voting officials either do not know the law or choose to ignore it.

The responsibility for the opinions expressed in this book rests with the authors who, in the spirit of free exchange of information, welcome any reader's corrections or comment.

Alan Reitman
New York, New York
April, 1972

v

Researcher's Acknowledgement

In any reference work, facts are gathered from a variety of sources, including prior compilations as well as primary source material. Innumerable individuals and groups lent their support to this undertaking. Dr. Constance E. Smith authored the original version of the book in 1960, and her text provided an invaluable reference point. Common Cause supplied most of the material used in the student voter section. The New York and National offices of the League of Women Voters provided source material used throughout the text. The Office of the General Counsel of the Department of the Army supplied a wealth of information used extensively in the sections on military voting. The Southern Regional Conference of Atlanta, Georgia, the Youth Citizenship Fund, Inc., the Republican and Democratic State Committees of New York, and the American Civil Liberties Union all contributed significantly.

Acknowledgement is also due Senator Thomas Eagleton of Missouri for information supplied in connection with electoral college reform, David Wells of the International Ladies Garment Workers Union for aid in the section on absentee voting, and William Boyd of the National Municipal League, whose information enhanced the section on apportionment. A special thanks is owed to the office of Senator Abraham Ribicoff of Connecticut for supplying invaluable material from the Legislative Reference Service of the Library of Congress, and to the library staff at Columbia University School of Law in New York for their able and willing assistance. Thanks is also owed to the Secretaries of State of the various states for their prompt and helpful responses to our inquiries.

While it would be impossible to list a complete bibliography of every source used in connection with the book, I would like to specially acknowledge two law review articles on which the section on Electoral College reform is largely based. They are: Buckles, "Electoral College Reform: The Proposals and Prospects," 14 St. Louis Univ. Law Journal 121 (1969); and Eagleton, "Direct Election vs. Vox Populi" 56 Amer. Bar Association Journal 543 (1970).

Robert B. Davidson
New York, New York
April, 1972

INTRODUCTION

In a democratic system of government the right to vote is probably the most fundamental of all rights. With it, the democratic experiment forged in the American Revolution, the idea of self-government, becomes a reality. Without it, the scheme under which the governed give consent to those who govern fails completely.

The selection of government leaders which occurs on Election Day, leaders who will create and administer policies that so pervasively affect the lives of citizens, is the most direct confrontation between the individual and government. It is the one way a citizen can actually control the course that government travels, the ultimate power that people possess in directing the operations of their government.

Even though it is not specified in the First Amendment's guarantee of freedom of speech, the right of franchise is closely linked to this vital constitutional protection. The exercise of franchise is surrounded by all sorts of political campaigning which rely on different forms of communication to win voters' support. By the casting of their ballots, individuals "speak" their heart and mind on candidates and public issues which can change the nation's path. In this view, voting, while not a right legally countenanced in the Bill of Rights, derives considerable backing from the notion of self-expression which the First Amendment advances.

This emphasis on voting as a right of expression does not diminish the social utility of periodic elections. How else can mistakes, wrong policies, abuses of power be checked? The cry of "throw the rascals out" is often criticized as personifying the fickleness of the electorate which simply desires a change of leaders, for the sake of seeing fresh faces at the helm of government. But the slogan also points up the value of the mechanism of voting by which people can correct erring policies that government has adopted.

Given the tremendous power that the franchise represents, it is little wonder that throughout the world the right to vote, which in our country is so often taken for granted (and so infrequently used*), was a prize fought for over centuries by people subject to tyrannical rule. This class struggle was waged in many different countries whose influence has shaped American life. Even today, in many parts of the globe where the struggle for self-determination continues relentlessly, the right to vote symbolizes that battle. This conflict is no stranger to the American scene. The right of suffrage was applied to women only 50 years ago when the 19th Amendment was adopted, a relatively short time span when measured against the long pages of history. And the fact that, in more recent times, the right to vote has been held by the courts to be constitutionally protected is no assurance that this right is enjoyed equally by all.

The contest over the right to vote has shifted from legal guarantees to making the right more meaningful, in the face of bitter opposition in many parts of the United States where the poor, black and brown Americans, the young and women are organizing their political power. The social revolution now being fought in the United States, to bring groups hitherto seen as outside the pale into society and to have them enjoy the rewards that others possess, is inextricably connected to exercising political power at the ballot box. One prime example is the rise of Negro voting power in the South where now more than 800 blacks hold public office, demonstrating the practical application of Martin Luther King's moral drive to awaken black citizens to their fundamental rights. (And when one remembers that the Constitution was finally adopted only through a compromise to count black slaves as only three-fifths of a person in apportioning Congressional representation, it is more than belated poetic justice to see Negro voters today assiduously courted by political leaders.)

But to assert the significance, Constitutional connection and pragmatic utility of the franchise is not enough to insure that this vast power will be fully and fairly exercised. For voting to be effective, it must be accompanied by safeguards that protect the independence of the voter as well as the integrity of the vote. Without such safeguards, a right of suffrage is meaningless. Yet in any social process as complex as elections, where the high

---

* According to the statistical Abstract of the United States, 1971, p. 364, in the 1970 elections, 75,976,000 persons registered to vote, 61.4% of the voting age population. And of these only 58,931,000 or 77.7% actually voted.

stakes of personal and political power are involved, candidates and parties may attempt to subvert this process in order to achieve their own interests and goals. Every election does reveal scattered instances of corruption and dishonesty, even a few which may alter the result of the election. But happily these have decreased markedly over the years, especially as the strength of big political machines has dwindled and voters have demonstrated a more independent turn of mind. Today it can fairly be claimed that American election results are on the whole free from serious distortion due to chicanery or downright fraud.

Fair elections are not achieved by the wave of a magic wand. A whole network of laws and procedures are at work to obtain this result. Voters can hardly be said to enjoy the voting privilege if they are victims of intimidation, whether by public officials, private groups or social pressures, and they are afraid to express their choice on the ballot. For the privilege to be meaningful the ballot must be a secret ballot and counted anonymously. Similarly, the voter must be protected against corruption and deliberate distortion of election results. Hence, the need for carefully-drawn registration requirements to prevent fraudulent voting, and strict legal limitations on the functions of election officials, including specified and detailed descriptions of their powers at every stage of the election process.

All of these are mere technical safeguards with little meaning unless the individual voter has the opportunity to exercise the right of choice. The voter must be presented with a ballot which lists genuine choices of candidates from which to make a selection. This is the distinguishing mark between elections in a free society and the trappings of elections in a totalitarian country where citizens are presented with only a single slate to rubber-stamp. The offering of alternatives is a major function of the American political party system, so the election codes of states contain numerous laws designed to encourage and protect the proper operation of the party machinery.

If election codes set forth an elaborate scheme for protecting the individual's right to vote, what about the other side of the coin, guarantees for society as a whole, to assure that informed and responsible people engage in the election process? State codes seek to achieve this by refusing to allow certain classes of people to vote--the idiot, the insane, and criminals-- and by establishing certain conditions for voting, such as age, residency and the ability to read and write. (The 1965 Voting

3

Rights Act, and subsequent Amendments, discussed on pp.144-5 describe recent changes in the three last-mentioned criteria.) While the objective is to guarantee an electorate capable of making rational decisions on matters of public interest, the fact is that far too often some of these requirements are subterfuges to curb political participation and preserve the political status quo. The wholesale reforms made in our federal and state laws within the past decade attest to the correctness of this characterization.

But laws are not always the determining factor in the election mix. As will be described in later portions of this book, many historical and technological developments in recent years have produced significant changes that drastically affect the election process. The phenomena of television as a potent campaign force, the demand for a major shake-up in the presidential nominating conventions to give the electorate a larger share in the selection process, and the soaring campaign costs which may limit choices of candidates to only the very rich are only some of the matters that must be reckoned with in considering the adequacy and equity of elections.

The vast changes that have marked the American scene in the past decade are no more sharply etched than in the American electoral system. We ordinarily think of the structure of this system as derived from our federal structure of government, with power distributed under the Constitution between the central government and various state governments. This power relationship has been altered considerably as the growing demand for personal rights and improved social conditions for disadvantaged groups pointed to the ballot box as the tool for social change. However, although states' authority in election matters has been reduced, there still are literally thousands of state laws which define voting, party organization, campaign procedures, nomination and the election machinery. These all reflect the deep involvement of states in the election process. Since each state legislature is virtually autonomous, the 50 state systems vary greatly. One must look at each of the state codes as well as the changes produced by the Congress and the courts to bring the American electoral system into proper focus.

Chapter 1

WHO HAS THE RIGHT TO VOTE?

Federal v. State Authority

Even a cursory reading of the Constitution discloses that each state seems to possess unquestioned authority over both the qualifications of persons selected to the Presidential Electoral College and the election machinery within the state's borders. Article II, Section 1 gives states the authority to determine the manner of appointing presidential electors. Article I, Section 4 grants to state legislatures the power to prescribe "the Times, Places and Manner of holding Elections for Senators and Representatives". Article I and the 17th Amendment (which provides for direct election of United States Senators), in declaring that people who vote for Senators or Representatives "shall have the Qualifications requisite for Electors of the most numerous Branch of the State Legislature", not only insure that a state cannot place greater restrictions on voting in federal elections than exist in statewide elections, but implicitly grant to the states the power to set their own qualifications for voters.

These provisions, coupled with each state's authority to supervise all elections for state office, appear to endow the states with decisive control over all elections. The fact that the Constitution, as part of Article I, Section 4, reserved to Congress the right to make or alter regulations for congressional or senatorial elections, "except as to the Places of choosing Senators", hardly downgrades state authority, for Congress has only rarely exercised this power and then only in very limited ways. Moreover, the Constitution also authorizes each state governor to call a special election when vacancies occur in congressional representation.

But the meaning of state constitutional provisions is always open to alteration by Supreme Court interpretation or amendment of the Constitution. Further change in constitutional edicts can result from congressional statutes, drawing on explications of the Constitution. All of these forces were activated in the last decade, primarily under the impetus of the various movements for major social reform. The result of three key developments

5

has been to temper the seemingly unrestricted power of the states. First, there was the adoption of certain constitutional amendments. In the initial voting change since the 19th Amendment in 1920 granted women the right to vote, Congress and the states approved the 24th and 26th Amendments, ending, in federal elections, the poll tax as a requirement for voting and lowering the voting age from 21 to 18. Second, reduction of state authority in voting matters was reinforced by passage of the major voting rights laws enacted by Congress in 1965 and 1970, especially the literacy and registration provisions, which drastically altered the shape of state legislative power over voting. Third, the Supreme Court contributed to the broadening of federal supremacy in voting by a number of decisions applying to various aspects of the franchise.

The power of states to specify who may vote was severely limited by the high court's interpretation of the 13th, 14th, and 15th Amendments, the so-called "Civil War Amendments". These three amendments, originally enacted in order to grant civil rights to newly-freed slaves, were repeatedly used to strike down state laws which directly or indirectly restricted minority Americans from gaining access to the ballot. The poll tax, literacy tests and related devices, and even to a great extent residency requirements, all fell in the face of constitutional attack. The 14th Amendment's proscription against any state law "which shall abridge the privileges or immunities of citizens of the United States" or which may "deny to any person within its jurisdiction the equal protection of the laws", proved to be one of the most potent weapons challenging state control of all elections.

The result of all this federal activity has been gradually to erode the states' power over voting to the point where it can now be stated that primary responsibility for insuring voting rights resides with the federal government.

Interestingly, the Constitution does not expressly and concretely define who shall have the right to vote. However, the lack of an affirmative declaration does not diminish the protection afforded individuals. Governmental power used to deny citizens the right to vote can be interdicted on the grounds noted above. Even a section of the 14th Amendment defining "citizens" as "all persons born or naturalized in the United States and subject to the jurisdiction thereof", can be seen as a positive protection of the right of franchise, since citizenship is in all states a requisite for suffrage.

6

Voter Qualifications

In view of the changes in federal-state relations affecting the franchise, examination of the state codes and federal legislation is necessary if one wants to understand fully the extent of the right to vote and how this right is now protected. At first glance the basic qualifications for voting on which state legislation is predicated seem direct, reasonable, and relatively simple for the average person to fulfill. On the whole, they are seldom arbitrary and seem to represent justifiable attempts to ensure an electorate with the maturity, mental capacity, and stake in the community to cast a responsible ballot. However, the federal actions alluded to in the preceeding section demonstrate how unsatisfactory these codes were in making the right to vote a reality for many Americans. Moreover, the state election codes are such a patchquilt that their bewildering array of minute provisions present obstacles which impede rather than facilitate voters' access to the polling booth.

Age

Since the beginning of World War II, there was considerable pressure for a constitutional amendment which would reduce the national voting age to 18. By 1960 only two states, Georgia and Kentucky, permitted 18-year olds to vote. Advocates of lowering the voting age continued to argue that a man who is old enough to face bullets is old enough to mark ballots--a difficult contention to refute, especially as the latest American military commitment, Vietnam, involved many thousands of young men who had not reached their maturity. Joined with the military argument was the claim that modern mass communication and transportation had so widened young peoples' bounds of knowledge that they were as informed as their elders on the issues of the day. The deep-felt involvement of high school and college students in social reform causes in the 1960's strengthened this argument and heightened the demand for lowering the voting age.

Finally, following the urging of several Presidents, the pressure of interested citizens' groups and the organization of youth itself, Congress, which has the sole power to enact a national law establishing for all states a revision in the voting age, took this significant step. Section 302 of the Votings Rights Act Amendments of 1970 specified an 18-yearold voting age in all elections. However, impediments to full-scale voting remained when the Supreme Court in its 1970 landmark decision, Oregon v. Mitchell, upheld the constitutionality of the federal statute only as applied to federal elections. But the high court's decision set the tone for further advance. A constitutional amendment extending the 18-year-old vote to state elections was approved by Congress, and finally ratified by the states on June 30, 1971.

The reduction of the voting age has touched off considerable speculation about the political impact of so many new voters on the political process. No one knows exactly what the result will be, but the sheer number of potential young voters points up their significance. The Voting Rights Act Amendments of 1970 and the 26th Amendment have added an estimated 11 million Americans to the list of prospective voters. This number would have been more than sufficient, for example, to have altered the popular vote outcome of every Presidential election in the nation's history, with the exception of Franklin Roosevelt's landslide victory over Alf Landon in 1936 and Lyndon Johnson's defeat of Barry Goldwater in 1964. According to political experts, however, only half of all young voters are expected to register and only two-thirds of these are expected to vote. But even this realistic analysis points up the enormous political ramifications of the lowered voting age. Given an estimated vote of 3.6 million among 18 to 21 year olds, this number would still have been sufficient to change the results of the 1960 and 1968 Presidential contests, where the victor's popular vote margin was 0.7% and 0.2%, respectively. These statistics may explain why in 1972 contenders for the Presidential nomination of both major parties expended so much energy and time in wooing the young voters.

But regardless of what role young people actually play in the 1972 Presidential elections, there are already signs that the influence of the 18-year-old vote is being felt or represents portents for the future. Many under or just-over-21 candidates are running for local political office, and some have been elected; young people are in the forefront of the campaigns for favorite presidential candidates. Perhaps of equal long-range importance, lowering of the voting age to 18 has led many states to lower the 21-age majority for entering into marriage and commercial contracts, for jury service and for exercising numerous other rights now enjoyed by persons over 21.

Citizenship

Citizenship is an unexceptionable requirement for voting in

8

every state. In addition to the broad provision of the 14th Amendment that a citizen is anyone born or naturalized in the United States, there are numerous laws dealing with special cases for the acquisition of citizenship. Anyone wishing to vote who is uncertain of his or her citizenship status should check with the Immigration and Naturalization Service of the United States Government (which has field offices in a number of major cities) to establish their exact standing, since the local registrar for elections in a community is not legally qualified to determine citizenship status. There are also non-governmental organizations, such as the American Immigration Conference, 509 Madison Avenue, New York City, and the American Council for Nationality Services, 20 West 40th Street, New York City, which can provide information. When applicants present themselves to the registrar, they must either take an oath that they are a natural-born citizen or present their original naturalization papers or a certified copy for the registrar's inspection before they can be registered as an elector. New citizens attempting to vote should be aware that three states require citizenship for specified time periods. In California and Utah, the registrant must have been a citizen for at least 90 days. Pennsylvania prescribes a 30-day minimum.

Residency

Every state code sets forth requirements specifying the length of time one must reside in the state, the county, and the election district before a person can register to vote. The underlying principle for all these stringent state regulations is clear: the assumption that only through living in a state for a specified period of time can a person become sufficiently conversant with local problems and candidates to vote intelligently. This prerequisite for voting not only prevents transients or migrants from participating in elections and possibly over-ruling the votes (and presumably the better judgment) of long-time residents, but also prevents fraud by providing a sufficient time period for registering (and verifying) voters and handling the other administrative details of the election process.

The idea of state residency requirements for specified time periods, however, came under sharp attack. Critics charged that such requirements were unnecessary and even unconstitutional. In view of the broadening channels of communication and the increased educational level of voters, information about issues and candidates, even local ones, can be easily obtained, certainly within a lesser period, such as 30 days. It was argued that a similar time was more than sufficient for handling the normal registration procedures. But the most important criticism heard was that a durational residency requirement restricted a citizen's right to travel freely from state to state. This restriction, in effect, amounted to a penalty for changing a residence prior to an election.

The problem was not insignificant, as statistics on the high mobility of the American people demonstrated. According to a report of the Bureau of the Census, about 18% of the national population, 36.2 million persons, moved during the March, 1970 - March 1971 period. The Bureau estimates that five and one-half million Americans are disfranchised each election because of their failure to fulfill state durational residency provisions. When county and district residency requirements are counted, the problem becomes more acute. In his book, "Principles of Demography" (1969), Donald Bogue estimated that one of every five persons was changing residence every year; 27.8 million were crossing county borders. Surprisingly, before the Voting Rights Act Amendments of 1970 were passed, only 29 states*took formal notice of the problem. They provided that a former state resident could vote in presidential elections in his or her old precinct for a specified length of time after moving to another location, if they could not qualify in their state of new residence, or that a new resident could vote in such elections even though the local residency requirements were not fulfilled.

Responding to the current realities of American life, both Congress and the courts acted to eliminate or reduce the impact of state durational residency requirements. In 1970 Congress abolished them for presidential elections. Section 202 of the Voting Rights Act Amendments of 1970 provides that no person will be denied the right to vote in a presidential election because of failure to fulfill state durational residency requirements. Every state must register a transient voter who applied up to 30 days before a presidential election. If a transient voter moves to another state within 30 days before the election, he or she may

* Alaska, Arizona, Colorado, Connecticut, Delaware, Florida, Hawaii, Illinois, Kansas, Louisiana, Maine, Maryland, Massachusetts, Michigan, Minnesota, Missouri, Nebraska, New Hampshire, New Jersey, New York, North Carolina, North Dakota, Ohio, Oklahoma, Oregon, Texas, Washington, Wisconsin and Wyoming,

now--in all states--obtain an absentee ballot up to a week before the election from the state of prior residency and cast that ballot in the presidential contest.

The Supreme Court, while initially dragging its feet, finally knocked out state residency requirements for all elections. But the all-embracing decision in the 1972 Dunn v. Blumstein case was not reached until after a lengthy court campaign involving a number of cases. In its 1965 Drueding v. Devlin ruling, the Supreme Court had upheld a one-year residency provision for voting in a presidential election. However, pressures for reconsideration mounted, with the focus on durational requirements for all elections. The results were mixed. United States District Courts had declared durational residency requirements unconstitutional in Tennessee, Indiana, Massachusetts, Minnesota, North Carolina, Alabama, Virginia, and Vermont, even though the same federal courts in Mississippi, Illinois, Washington, Louisiana, Ohio, Arizona, and Wisconsin had ruled just the opposite. And while the Voting Rights Act Amendments solved the problem of residency standards in presidential elections, the Supreme Court, in its 1971 Oregon v. Mitchell decision approving Congress' authority to pass laws banning state durational residency requirements, did not tackle the question of whether such requirements were unconstitutional.

This barrier was broken in the 1972 decision which concerned a Tennessee citizen's challenge of that state's one-year residency requirement. In its opinion, the high court held the one-year requirement invalid as a violation of the equal protection clause, largely as a consequence of several non-voting decisions favoring freedom of interstate travel. (The right to travel, although nowhere specifically mentioned in the Constitution, is often said to find its constitutional under-pinnings in the 14th Amendment's prohibition against any state law which "abridges the privileges or immunities of citizens"). In 1966, the Supreme Court held, in part, in U.S. v. Guest, that restricting a citizen's right to travel freely from state to state was a deprivation of civil rights and thus amounted to a crime under federal law. In 1969, the Supreme Court declared, in Shapiro v. Thompson, that the government could not impose residency requirements on a person as a condition for receiving welfare benefits. The Court reasoned that the right to travel was a "fundamental" right and could only be abridged if the state showed that it had a compelling interest for doing so. This same rationale was used in the Blumstein decision. As Justice Thurgood Marshall stated:

Durational residency laws impermissibly condition and penalize the right to travel by imposing their prohibitions on only those persons who have recently exercised that right. In the present case, such laws force a person who wishes to travel and change residences to choose between travel and the basic right to vote. Absent a compelling state interest, a State may not burden the right to travel in this way.

While the Supreme Court did not fix a permissible time period in the Blumstein case, it did say "that 30 days appears to be an ample period of time" for a state to guard against election fraud. The pre-Blumstein durational requirements can be noted on the chart at page 101.While it is still too early to define precisely the impact of the Blumstein decision, it is certain that lengthy durational residence requirements, like so many other burdens on the franchise, are remnants of the past, having fallen before the commands of the Constitution's equal-protection guarantee.

Defining Residency for Voting Purposes

Quite apart from the durational residency requirements, the ability of people to vote can be affected by the definition of residency. Most codes very carefully define the term. Residence refers to the voter's permanent abode, to the location from which there is intention to return after temporary absence. For a married person, the place where the family resides is usually considered the residence unless either spouse is separated and maintains a separate home. For a single person, the place where he or she sleeps is usually regarded as the residence. Two residences cannot be listed, for as soon as one place is recorded, the right to claim a second is relinquished. For military personnel and related groups, the Federal Voting Assistance Act of 1955 states that legal residence

is generally considered the state from which the person entered military service, left the territorial United States in the service of the Federal Government, or left in the service of a religious group or welfare agency assisting members of the Armed Forces.

An elector does not lose residence because he or she is temporarily absent from the home. (In most states the law declares that confinement to prison or to a charitable institution or asylum does not deprive one of residence rights, but persons confined to mental or penal institutions are generally not allowed to register and those in charitable institutions are almost never granted the franchise.) All election codes specifically state that residence is not lost by a person who is serving in the armed forces or in agencies providing services for the armed forces; most codes further provide that electors who are absent because they work for the state or federal government, or are employed in navigation in inland waterways, or who are attending a school, college, university or other institution of higher learning, retain their residence rights.

It should be noted, however, that just as one does not lose residence while engaged in these pursuits, for two large segments of the population--military personnel and students--there is growing controversy over whether state residency can be acquired by virtue of being stationed at a military establishment or by being a resident student within the state. The issue is not one of losing totally the right of franchise, as state laws provide absentee ballots for servicemen, their spouses and dependents, and students. Instead, the argument revolves around whether members of the Armed Forces and students can make their right to vote effective, by voting in places where they presently reside and thus have an impact on the conditions of their life in those communities and states. Since career servicemen are stationed at military bases indefinitely and students spend at least four years at institutions of higher learning, this comment is frequently heard: can they really be regarded as transients undeserving of equal treatment, along with other newcomers who establish voting residence. The problem is not an illusory one nor lacking legal complexities. By 1970, 24 states had laws on their statute books which, in effect, asserted that no one gains or loses a residency for purpose of voting because he or she resides at a military installation or institution of higher learning. It is important to emphasize that restrictive state practices affecting military personnel apply only to persons residing within a military installation. In all states, members of the armed forces living off-base may qualify to vote in the same manner as any other state resident.

Indicative of the drive to liberalize the right of franchise, the Supreme Court and the Congress have moved to ease state restrictions affecting members of the armed forces. In its 1965 Carrington v. Rash decision, the Supreme Court voided a Texas statute which effectively barred resident military personnel from voting in local elections. The Court held that the state must at least give any person who wished to establish a permanent residence an opportunity to present evidence as to his domicile. Three years later, in the interest of removing all legal obstacles to military people residing on a military installation, Congress enacted Public Law 90-344 which suggested to the states that a military family be allowed to change its state of legal residence if it so desired, even though all or part of a residency requirement was fulfilled while the family resided on a military installation.

Thirteen states, including many with significant military populations (Mississippi, Georgia, South Carolina, and Texas), have enacted laws permitting on-base residents to qualify in their state of military assignment, often after some additional proof or declaration that the military voter intends to remain permanently in the state. Two states, Nevada and Utah, permit only spouses and dependents of on-base military residents to qualify to vote, on the theory that unlike their husbands or fathers, spouses and dependents are "voluntary" residents who by their presence have evidenced an intent to make the state their permanent home.

The problem has been further eased by the Supreme Court's 1970 Evans v. Cornman decision which held that an otherwise qualified voter, who is regarded as a resident of the state, cannot be denied the franchise solely because he or she resides on a federal enclave.

Although reform steps have opened the doors to increased voting by resident military personnel, students have to face much stiffer opposition in claiming the right to vote in places of residency. On the surface there are differences. Students are considered more transient than military personnel because of vacations, the usual summer recess, and flexible educational programs which feature spending a semester or year at different colleges and universities. But a more likely explanation is the conservative cast of most state legislatures and their fear of student voting power.*

While the rationale of the Supreme Court's Carrington v. Rash decision by implication forbids a state from arbitrarily excluding students from local voter lists, subtle (and not so subtle) forms of discrimination have been practiced. Registrars have refused to place students on registration rolls without some im-

---

*The legislators fear is not without cause. In Massachusetts, students have the power to control at least seven communities. In the same state, students comprise more than 10% of the total number of potential voters in 17 localities. Similar situations

possible-to-obtain definitive proof--such as property owner-
ship--of their intention to remain permanently within the voting
district.   University of Alabama students were blocked from
voting in the 1968 election when the Tuscaloosa Board of Registrars required the completion of a "Voter Registration Student
Questionnaire"; this provided an excuse for failing to register
students pending "evaluation" of the forms. Initially, California's
Attorney General ruled that unmarried students must, in general,
vote in their parent's precinct. In New York, the state legislature
recently made it almost impossible for all but a few students to
register where they go to school by empowering local election
officials to consider among voting qualifications for students the
residency of parents.

    Efforts to stymie student voting have not gone unchallenged,
primarily on the ground of discriminatory treatment. States that
make student voters fill out special forms, or answer a special
questionnaire, or produce documentation not required of other
registrants, violate the 14th Amendment's equal protection clause
by effectively discriminating against these new voters solely because they are students.   In addition, the federal voting law
(1971 (a)(2)(A) of Title 42 of the United States Code) prohibits
any administrative officer from applying to any otherwise qualified individual "any standard, practice, or procedure different
from the standards, practices, or procedures applied under such
voting laws to any other individuals." The legal challenges also
rest on the newly-ratified 26th Amendment to the Constitution
which states that:

    The right of citizens of the United States, who are eighteen
    years of age or older, to vote shall not be denied or abridged

    by the United States or by any State on account of age.
The language of the Amendment is broad enough, it is felt, to
cover localities which discriminate against students who wish to
register in their college towns. The 1970 Census, which is used
to apportion Congressional representation, also has been cited
as precedent for recognizing students' residency in their college
community for voting purpose. The Bureau of the Census counted

---

exist in many college towns. In Champaign, Illinois, for example,
16,000 votes are cast at a usual election--the same as the number
of students who live at the University of Illinois. The concen-
tration of students in certain communities presupposes that students will vote as a bloc. While this may be true in certain communities, many analysts believe that the student vote will be
divided according to their home background and parents' voting
pattern.

the college locality as a student's place of residency, not the parent's home district.

The heavy controversy stirred by the student voting problem has led to a flurry of court decisions and state attorney general opinions. The response has been mixed, but the trend seems to be toward qualifying students to vote in their college or university site of residence.

Before the 26th Amendment was ratified on June 30, 1971, only six states (Alaska, Colorado, Nebraska, Utah, Washington, and Wisconsin) permitted students to register in their college town. Presently, 22 states now allow students to register in exactly the same manner as all other voter applicants, including many with significant college populations (Massachusetts, Michigan, Connecticut, Illinois and Pennsylvania). And five other states permit students to vote in their college communities after some questioning designed to verify the student's expressed intention to make the college town his or her permanent residency. Chart B, compiled by Common Cause, a citizens lobby which provided leadership to the student voter movement, supplies the details. The reader should consult the chart key in order to understand the distinctions among the states (see p. 104).

Literacy and Related Tests

There can be no quarrel that literacy is a desirable condition for creating an informed and responsible electorate. A voter able to read and write is in a better position to evaluate candidates and issues, by reviewing newspapers and television political coverage and party campaign materials, than if he or she were dependent on word-of-mouth recommendations or hearsay about political figures. If voters are literate there is greater possibility that they will exercise independent thinking about candidates and issues. And independent political attitudes go hand-in-hand with freedom from political domination.

Originally, literacy tests were adopted to try to avoid the corruption of political machines. Some of the northern states (Connecticut in 1855 and Massachusetts in 1875) sought to prevent voting by new immigrants who, because of their inability to read or write, were thought susceptible to the favors of political bosses. But the focus of literacy tests changed after adoption in 1870 of the 15th Amendment, which removed color, race and previous servitude as conditions for voting. Southern states seized on these tests as a device to thwart voting by the "freed" blacks who, in their previous slave status, had been denied such rudiments of education as reading and writing.

The historical record shows that state attempts to enfranchise only the "literate" ranged from a requirement that the applicant be able to read or write English or his mother tongue, to one that the potential elector be able to read any section of the state or federal constitution and demonstrate understanding of it. An obvious drawback to provisions which required a voter to show understanding or give a reasonable interpretation of a section of a constitution (as the Louisiana and Mississippi statutes required) was the difficulty of establishing fair and sound criteria for the determination of "understanding". When such evaluation fell within the discretionary power of the registrar (as it did in North Carolina where the statute declared it the duty of the local registrar to "administer" the literacy tests), it was almost impossible to ensure uniform treatment of registrants throughout the state. Any evaluative system lacking specific standards for determining success and failure is subject to the partiality of the person giving the test. New York evolved probably the best answer to this problem by placing literacy testing in the hands of the Board of Regents which provided an official examination that was graded objectively. The elector who could not produce evidence of educational attainment was required to pass such a test. In Georgia, on the other hand, the alternative test for the person who could not read or write contained a set of 30 standard questions of which the illiterate voter orally had to answer 20 in order to qualify to vote. The detailed questions (What is the definition of a felony in Georgia? Who is the solicitor general of the State Judicial Circuit in which you live and who is the judge of such circuit? What are the names of the persons who occupy the following offices in your county: Clerk of the Superior Court, Ordinary, Sheriff?) obviously were extraordinarily difficult for the generally well-informed and presumably well-qualified voter to answer, to say nothing of the illiterate.

The initiation of literacy and related tests as a device to thwart voting by blacks in Southern states is clearly depicted in this excerpt from a 1965 report by 12 members of the Judiciary Committee of the United States Senate:

Prior to 1890, apparently no Southern State required proof of literacy, understanding of constitutional provisions or of obligations of citizenship, or good moral character, as prerequisites for voting. However, as the following table shows, these tests and devices were soon to appear in most of the States with large Negro populations.

1. Reading and/or writing: Mississippi (1890), South Carolina (1895), North Carolina (1900), Alabama (1901), Vir-

17

ginia (1902), Georgia (1908), Louisiana (1921). And see Oklahoma (1910).

2. Completion of an application form: Louisiana (1898), Virginia (1902), Louisiana (1921), Mississippi (1954).

3. Oral constitutional "understanding" and "interpretation" tests: Mississippi (1890), South Carolina (1895), Virginia (1902), Louisiana (1921).

4. Understanding of the duties and obligations of citizenship: Alabama (1901), Georgia (1908), Louisiana (1921), Mississippi (1954).

5. Good moral character requirement (other than nonconviction of a crime): Alabama (1901), Georgia (1908), Louisiana (1921), Mississippi (1960).

It is significant that in 1890, 69 percent or more of the adult Negroes in seven Southern States which adopted these tests were illiterate (Alabama, 78 percent; Louisiana, 77 percent; Georgia, 75 percent; Mississippi, 74 percent; South Carolina, 73 percent; North Carolina, 70 percent; Virginia, 69 percent). These percentages were very much higher than comparable figures for white illiteracy (Alabama, 19 percent; Louisiana 19 percent; Georgia, 17 percent; Mississippi, 13 percent; South Carolina, 18 percent; North Carolina, 25 percent; Virginia, 15 percent).

The unabashed discriminatory purpose of such tests was marked in the laws that many southern states adopted exempting illiterate whites. White voters in Louisiana, North Carolina and Oklahoma were exempted by a "voting grandfather clause" which permitted lineal descendants of early voters to vote without taking such a test. Other exceptions flowed from property ownership (Louisiana, Alabama, Virginia, Georgia and South Carolina); being a person "of good moral character" who understood the "duties and obligations of citizenship under a republican form of government" (Alabama and Georgia); or could satisfy the registrar that a person could "understand" and "interpret" a constitutional text when it was read to them (Mississippi, South Carolina, Virginia and Louisiana). The grandfather clause was voided by the Guinn v. U.S. Supreme Court decision in 1915, but the other devices remained.

While literacy provisions in state election laws were revised and refined from time to time, states which did not have them showed little interest in adopting these tests. Undoubtedly the national decrease in immigration since the 1920's and the spread of compulsory public education tended to lower desire for such tests. By 1960, fewer than half the states administered literacy

18

tests to voters, and most of these were in the South, where the purpose remained to impede the Negro registrant. However, under the massive pressures built up by the advocates of civil rights, even the legal restrictions in Southern states were swept away.

The civil rights movement pinpointed voting reform as a prime target and eventually succeeded in ending literacy tests as a qualification for voting. But the struggle was not an easy one. The first round was unsuccessfully fought in the Supreme Court which, in its 1959 Lassiter v. Northhampton County Board of Elections decision, rejected a frontal attack on literacy requirements. The Court held that the 14th Amendment did not forbid literacy tests as long as they were administered in a nondiscriminatory manner.

The battleground then shifted to the Congress where major breakthroughs occurred in the Civil Rights Acts of 1957, 1960, and 1964. Interference with a person's exercise of voting rights was made a federal crime, but the enforcement provisions were weak. Although these laws authorized suits to redress denials of the right to vote on grounds of race or color, the burden was on the aggrieved party who had to bear the burden of months, or even years, of litigation (and community intimidation) simply to obtain the right to vote. Literacy tests began to crumble when the 1964 law barred states from using such tests in registering persons for federal elections unless the tests were administered and conducted wholly in writing. The statute also established the presumption that a voter was literate if he had completed six grades of education.

But the key victory was scored in the Voting Rights Act of 1965. The method of enforcing voting rights was revamped by adoption of the controversial "automatic trigger" provision. This section automatically suspended all literacy tests and related deviced in any "political subdivision" when two conditions occurred: (1) the Attorney General decided that such a test or device was used by November 1, 1964; and (2) the Director of the Census determined by the same date that less than 50% of eligible voters were actually registered, or that less than 50% of those eligible actually voted in the 1964 presidential election.

The results were dramatic. Under the "automatic trigger" provision, all literacy tests and devices were eliminated in six southern states--Alabama, Georgia, Louisiana, Mississippi, South Carolina and Virginia--and in 39 counties of North Carolina. Negro registration soared, with the help of federal registrars authorized in the 1965 Act and various black and student organizations who saw that the road to political power and social change depended in large measure on the growth of the black franchise. (See Chapter 2 for further details on techniques used for increasing registration of blacks.) The federal courts also proved a helpful ally by their rulings on voting discrimination suits. More than 200 suits have been brought since 1965, either by the Department of Justice or private parties, with the court increasingly accepting federal jurisdiction, finding certain practices constituted discrimination and ordering the discrimination to cease. The following chart, taken from a 1968 report of the U.S. Civil Rights Commission, points up the significant gains made in seven deep-South States.

Percent of Non-White Registration*

State	Prior to Voting Rights Act of 1965	Spring-Summer 1968
Alabama	19.3	56.7
Georgia	27.4	56.1
Louisiana	31.6	59.3
Mississippi	6.7	59.4
North Carolina	46.8	55.3
South Carolina	37.3	50.8
Virginia	38.3	58.4

* Later figures compiled on the basis of the 1970 Census are not yet available

A number of Southern states, realizing that political power alignments would be dramatically shifted by the federal law, attacked its constitutionality, primarily on the basis that the states, not the federal government, have ultimate control over the qualifications of electors. However, the Supreme Court rejected this contention in its 1966 South Carolina v. Katzenbach decision validating the federal government's right to preempt state authority in this area. Opponents of the federal law did not cease their attacks. As late as 1970, Congress rejected an attempt to alter the "automatic trigger formula" approach. The target was a section of the 1965 Act, as extended in 1970, which provides that none of the states covered by the trigger formula may change their voting laws and procedures without first submitting the proposed change to a three-judge federal court in the District of Columbia or the Attorney General. No change can be made unless the Attorney General approves it within 60 days or the three-judge court rules that the revision will not abridge anyone's right to vote because of race or color. Under the Supreme Court's South Carolina v. Katzenbach decision, it is up to the states or the political subdivision to persuade the Attorney General or the courts that the proposed change is not discriminatory.

In 1971 the Department of Justice sought, by an administrative ruling, to circumvent the Congressional statute. It proposed that when a state submits a voting law change to the Attorney General, and he is unable to decide whether the new statute would be discriminatory, the state or subdivision will be given the benefit of the doubt and the new law would be allowed. In effect, the burden of proof would shift from the states to the Attorney General, and if he thought he couldn't decide the issue--for example, because of the time element or the complex facts--then the state would be free to go ahead, even if later events proved some citizens were disfranchised. Fortunately, the Department's plan came to public attention, vigorous protests were registered and the idea was dropped.

Another Supreme Court ruling involving the literacy concept stemmed from a provision of the 1965 law which made a sixth-grade education in a non-English speaking American-flag-school a conclusive presumption of literacy. This section offered the promise of increased voting in urban centers, especially among many Spanish-speaking Americans who hitherto had been denied the right to vote because of their failure to pass New York's English literacy requirement. The high court's 1966 Katzenbach v. Morgan decision upheld the constitutionality of the sixth-grade test and is especially significant because of its implication that the federal government possessed constitutional authority to enforce, by any means determined "appropriate", the

21

command of the 15th Amendment that "The rights of citizens of the United States to vote shall not be abridged. . .on account of race, color, or previous condition of servitude."

Despite the suspension of literacy tests in many southern states, the drive for total abolition continued. This goal apparently was attained in the Voting Rights Act Amendments of 1970 which suspended literacy tests in all states until August 6, 1975. This was achieved by continuing the 1965 Act's time limit on suspension of tests for five more years and by extending coverage to all states, not just those affected by the "automatic trigger". While it was hoped in 1965 that five years would be enough time in which to remedy this most odious aspect of discriminatory voting practices, experience proved otherwise. Recalcitrant southern voting officials utilized numerous harassing techniques to circumvent the clear aim of the law. (See Chapter 2 for details.) A 1970 House of Representatives Report (No. 91-397) cited this gloomy evidence in urging extension of the ban on literacy tests and devices.

[A] substantial number of counties still disclose extremely low Negro registration. For example, in Alabama less than 50 percent of Negroes of voting age are registered in 27 of 67 counties; in five counties, Negro registration is less than 35 percent; in Georgia, less than 50 percent of Negroes of voting age are registered in 68 of 162 counties; in 27 counties it is less than 35 percent; in Mississippi, less than 50 percent of Negroes of voting age are registered in 24 of 82 counties; in six counties it is less than 35 percent; in South Carolina, less than 50 percent of Negroes of voting age are registered in 23 of 46 counties; in three counties it is less than 35 percent.

Although these figures deal only with southern states, many northern states imposed literacy tests until the 1970 Voting Act amendments. Twelve out of the 19 states whose tests were suspended by the amendments were outside the South: Alaska, Arizona, California, Connecticut, Delaware, Maine, Massachusetts, New Hampshire, New York, Oregon, Washington, and Wyoming.

Even though these statistics point up how much more remains to be done to implement the objective of the federal ban on literacy tests and devices, a Supreme Court decision in a related field may alleviate the problems. In its 1969 Gaston County v. United States decision, the Court held that any jurisdiction which maintained a segregated and inferior school system

22

for its voting-age Negro residents could not reinstitute a literacy test as a prerequisite to voting. The high court said that this would have the effect of denying Negroes the right to vote on account of race or color.

In a different area of literacy, virtually all states have laws to assist illiterate electors when they vote. To avoid undue political influence, the voter requiring assistance is aided by two election officials representing different parties. Voters who are prevented from reading or writing by physical disabilities or blindness are allowed to vote under certain special arrangements. Some of these special arrangements are described in Chapter 3, "How does the Voting System Work?"

Poll Taxes

Today, after years of hard, but successful, campaigning for major legislative voting reforms, the idea of paying a tax in order to vote seems far-fetched. Indeed it has been totally outlawed by a constitutional amendment, Congressional action, and Supreme Court interpretation.

Yet only a decade ago the payment of a poll tax remained a prerequisite to voting in five southern states: Alabama, Arkansas, Mississippi, Texas and Virginia. Vermont also had a poll tax requirement applicable only to local elections. The annual tax in these states was not exorbitant. It ranged from $1.00 in Arkansas to $2.00 in Mississippi. The tax rates and cumulative provisions, i.e., how much infrequent voters who skipped elections could be compelled to pay "back taxes", are described in the following table from a report of the House of Representatives, prepared as part of the legislative history of the Voting Rights Act of 1965. Arkansas is excluded from the chart because by 1965 it had passed a constitutional amendment abolishing the poll tax.

States Requiring Poll Tax, 1960

State	Annual Rate	Cumulative Provision	Maximum Charge	Maximum additional tax at option of local authorities
Alabama	$1.50	2 yrs.	$3.00	None
Mississippi	2.00	2 yrs.	4.00	$1.00 counties[1]
Texas	1.50	None	1.50	$0.25 counties[2] $1.00 cities[3]
Virginia	1.50	3 yrs.	4.50[4]	$1.00 cities $1.00 towns [1]

[1] Local areas have not made use of their authority to levy poll taxes.
[2] All counties levy this.
[3] Some cities require payment of an additional tax of $1.00 as a prerequisite for voting in municipal elections.
[4] With penalties, the maximum possible payment is $5.01 per person.

Although the alleged purpose of the poll tax was to raise revenue and discourage voting by disinterested individuals, it was generally recognized that the tax was a device to disfranchise thousands of citizens, many of them black. The low economic status of southern Negroes and the psychological hurdle that the poll tax symbolized for people afraid of asserting their rights formed an effective barrier to voting by large numbers of blacks in these states.

However, as the civil rights movement of the 1960's captured public attention and interest, eliminating the poll tax became a primary goal of those seeking strong federal action in the field of racial discrimination. The effort culminated in the 24th Amendment to the Constitution, ratified in 1964, which abolished poll taxes in federal elections.

The poll tax remained as an impediment to voting in state elections, and this problem was recognized by Congress during its debate on the Voting Rights Act of 1965. In the original version of the Act, the Senate Judiciary Committee recommended a provision outlawing the poll tax in all elections, but objections from southern states produced a compromise. The final bill, while not specifically outlawing the tax, contained a Congressional "declaration of policy". The following text makes it strikingly clear that Congress regarded the tax as a scheme to impair voting rights.

(a) The Congress finds that the requirement of the payment of a poll tax as a precondition to voting (i) precludes persons of limited means from voting or imposes unreasonable financial hardship upon such persons as a precondition to their exercise of franchise, (ii) does not bear a reasonable relationship to any legitimate State interest in the conduct of elections, and (iii) in some areas has the purpose or effect of denying persons the right to vote because of race or color. Upon the bases of these findings, Congress declares that the constitutional right of citizens to vote is denied or abridged in some areas by the requirement of the payment of a poll tax as a precondition to voting.

The 1965 law also authorized the Attorney General to bring a legal action enjoining state enforcement of a poll tax requirement and provided that such suits would come under the jurisdiction of a three-judge Federal District Court. This meant appeals could be taken directly to the Supreme Court, thereby speeding up the adjudicatory process. This special provision was applied in 1966 when the Department of Justice instituted suit against enforcement of Virginia's poll tax. And in the case of Harper v. Virginia Board of Elections, the Supreme Court sounded the final death knell of the poll tax when it ruled Virginia's requirement unconstitutional. The Court reasoned that because payment of the tax had no relation to the intelligent casting of a ballot, it worked an invidious discrimination against the poor and was thus violative of the equal protection clause of the 14th Amendment.

Property Ownership

For many years the ownership of property was a requisite for voting in most elections. But today such a qualification is rarely found in election codes. The property ownership rationale rested upon the desire to prevent irresponsible voting on financial issues which may materially affect the tax rates of a community. But a series of judicial decisions indicate that property ownership as the basis for voting is evidence of class-economic bias, a hold-over from our earlier history, and offends the growing constitutional concept of equal protection under law.

The Supreme Court, in its 1969 Kramer v. Union Free School District No. 15 decision, invalidated a New York statute which restricted voters in school district elections to those who (1) owned or leased taxable real property; or (2) were parents or had custody of children enrolled in the local public schools. Ruling that New York's classification, based in part on property ownership, was too broad, the Court noted that:

> The classifications. . .permit inclusion of many persons who have, at best, a remote and indirect interest in school affairs and, on the other hand, exclude others who have a distinct and direct interest in the school meeting decisions.

Although this explanation left open the possibility of a property ownership requirement where appropriately imposed, subsequent Supreme Court cases further discouraged this notion.

Also in 1969, in the case of Cipriano v. City of Houma, the Court struck down a Louisiana statute restricting the right to vote in municipal bond elections to "property taxpayers". Its opinion asserted that:

> The challenged statute contains a classification which excludes otherwise qualified voters who are as substantially affected and directly interested in the matter voted upon as are those who are permitted to vote. When, as in this case, the State's sole justification for the statute is that the classification provides a 'rational basis' for limiting the franchise to those voters with a 'special interest', the statute clearly does not meet the 'exacting standard of precision' we require of statutes which selectively distribute the franchise.

The Court's "standard of precision" is that when fundamental rights such as voting are involved, the state must show not simply a "rational basis" for its statutory classification (in Cipriano and Kramer, property vs. nonproperty owners), but a compelling state interest for maintaining the property ownership criterion.

Still another high court ruling cut even more deeply through the barriers that property ownership placed in the way of voting. In the 1970 Phoenix v. Kolodziejski decision, Arizona's restricting the franchise in general obligation bond elections to real property taxpayers was invalidated. Of the 13 other states which confined voting in some or all general bond elections to real property owners or property taxpayers, only four--Michigan, New York, Rhode Island, and Texas--still retain this standard. Courts in five states--Florida, Louisiana, New Mexico, Oklahoma and Utah--have declared the requirement unconstitutional as a violation of equal protection, and four other states--Alaska,

Colorado, Idaho and Montana--have repealed their restrictive laws through legislation or constitutional amendment.

Taken all together, the decisions appear to doom property ownership as a precondition to voting. Like the poll tax and, to some extent, literacy tests, property ownership is a remnant of early America when affluence and formal education were regarded as the best measuring rods to judge those privileged to exercise voting rights. Time has marched on and the classification of wealth is properly subject to the most searching judicial scrutiny to determine if it evidences discriminatory treatment. As Chief Justice Earl Warren stated in the Kramer case,

> Any unjustified discrimination in determining who may participate in political affairs or in the selection of public officials undermines the legitimacy of representative government.

Voter Disqualifications

The accelerating pace of voting reform which has swelled the size of the electorate among the young and racial and ethnic minorities has not affected other groups regarded as outside society's pale and undeserving of rights. The theory is that the caliber of the electorate must be protected against so-called undesirables, by explicitly barring them from taking part in elections.

Despite the general trend away from untrammeled state authority in voting matters, where voter disqualifications are concerned, the law of each state is supreme. Voter disqualifications are generally divided into three major headings: the insane, the indigent, and criminals.

All persons determined to be mentally unsound, idiots, and insane, and those under legal guardianship, are almost always denied the right to vote on the ground that such individuals are incapable of rendering a rational decision in the voting booth. Forty-five states disqualify such persons. Only Michigan, New Hampshire, Pennsylvania, Texas and Vermont do not disqualify such persons. Alaska adds the provision that the voter must be judicially determined to be of unsound mind.

Disfranchisement of indigents is legitimatized in seven states. (Delaware, Massachusetts, Missouri, Rhode Island, South Carolina, Texas, and West Virginia.) The main reason for refusing the vote to paupers is the same as the fallacious property-ownership notion, that intelligent decision-making is related to economic status. The argument also has been made that an indigent voter may be susceptible to bribery with the cure for this evil being preventing paupers from voting. This contention reflects the lingering but sharp class feeling that those who contribute so little economically to the community should be denied the right to select governmental officials, a position that is out of harmony with the idea of self-government.

However, economic means tests as a condition for voting may be waning. In view of Supreme Court decisions that a person's pecuniary status does not bar him or her from the guarantees of the 14th Amendment's equal protection clause, the realization that poverty is a national social problem which must be eradicated, and the rising political power of organized poverty groups, the trend is definitely away from tying a voter's economic level to the right to enter the voting booth. Even in the seven states which specifically disqualify "paupers" as voting registrants, the term is differently defined. Delaware, Rhode Island, West Virginia and Massachusetts simply exclude "paupers" from the franchise, with Massachusetts making an exception for war veterans confined in a state institution. This designation appears only to include those traditionally known as "paupers", i.e. those under public charge. Several other states, however, are more specific. Missouri and Texas disqualify any person kept at any poorhouse or other asylum at public expense, and Missouri's disqualification includes all paupers "except [those confined at] the federal sailors' home at St. James." South Carolina disfranchises paupers and then adds the express provision that a person receiving public aid or assistance shall not be considered a pauper.

Acting on the proposition that voting is a right belonging only to law-abiding citizens, a natural concomitant of the desire for a responsible electorate, 45 states forbid criminals from voting. The five other states are Arkansas, Maine, Massachusetts, Pennsylvania and Vermont. The last three named do disqualify only persons convicted of certain election offenses, such as bribery and corrupt practices.

In recent years criticism of the disfranchisement of convicted criminals has grown. This stems from the rising public awareness of the inadequacies and injustices of our criminal justice system. As efforts developed to change the prison system and make it more responsive to basic human needs, regaining of the franchise joined the list of reformist demands, along with non-censorship of reading materials, more frequent and private

28

visits with attorneys and family, freedom of religion, and an end to physical abuse.

The criticism rests on two grounds. First, the states' stripping of voting rights from all convicted felons is not rationally related to protecting the purity of the election process; disfranchisement for committing crimes affecting elections would seem to be sufficient.* Second, prohibiting ex-convicts from voting makes their adjustment to society more difficult and conflicts with modern penology's emphasis on advancing rehabilitation by not heaping civil disabilities on the ex-felon once his or her debt to society has been paid. So far this position has had tough sledding in the courts. The U.S. Court of Appeals for the Second Circuit in 1967 rejected these arguments in the case of Green v. Board of Elections of the City of New York, stating that:

> A contention that the equal protection clause requires New York to allow convicted mafiosi to vote for district attorneys or judges would not only be without merit, but as obviously as anything can be.

The U.S. Supreme Court refused to review this case, but in its 1969 Beacham v. Braterman decision took a stronger position, by affirming a Florida court ruling upholding that state's power to disfranchise felons otherwise qualified to vote. In the 1970's, as the prison reform drive steps up its pace, new challenges can be expected.

Despite the courts' present reluctance to re-institute the right to vote for ex-prisoners, 42 states have procedures for restoring a felon's civil rights, including the right to vote. (In addition to the five states which do not disfranchise criminals, Delaware, Mississippi, and West Virginia do not provide for restoration of a felon's right to vote.) In most states, among them Illinois, Kentucky, Montana and Virginia, the governor has the power to restore a former convict to full civil rights; in other states, such as Connecticut, a special commission pos-

---

* Such election crimes as bribery or voting fraud are understandably reprehensible. Twenty-one states, Alabama, Delaware, Florida, Hawaii, Idaho, Illinois, Iowa (only election officials), Kentucky, Maryland, Massachusetts, Missouri, New Hampshire, New Jersey, New York, Ohio, Pennsylvania, South Carolina, Utah, Vermont, West Virginia and Wisconsin -- expressly disfranchise persons for conviction of certain election offenses. In most of the other states, the definition of "felon" will have the same effect.

sesses the right, and in Rhode Island an act of the General Assembly is required to restore voting rights. In Colorado, Hawaii and Oregon, felons regain the franchise immediately upon release from prison. Felons may vote in New York if the maximum sentence has expired or the individual has completed parole. In Michigan felons are not directly disfranchised, but the same result is accomplished by defining them as outside the "absent elector" statute.

But the existence of procedures to give back the franchise is not tantamount to automatic restoration. And many states still impose prohibitions which seem unfair. In Texas, for example, all felons lose the right to vote. Breaking and entering a coin-operated machine is defined as a felony, as is the crime of conspiring to commit a felony. Thus, conspiring to rifle a penny-gum machine could result in the loss of the right to vote.

Voter disqualifications in 32 states reach beyond the traditional categories (indigent, insane, criminals) to mark those felt to be unfit to cast a ballot. Persons who duel are expressly disfranchised in California, Florida, Mississippi, Nevada, South Carolina, Texas and Virginia. Bad moral character disqualifies a voter in Alabama, Connecticut, Georgia, Louisiana, and Mississippi; the prevalence of this standard in southern states undoubtedly relates to the ill defined "character" tests and other devices used before the 1965 Voting Rights Act to discriminate against black voters. Other discriminatory categories include betting on elections (Florida), engaging in a variety of sexual practices (Idaho), participating in "subversive activities" (Washington), and being dishonorably discharged from the armed forces (Louisiana and West Virginia).

Chapter 2

HOW IS REGISTRATION HANDLED?

The Importance of Registration

A fundamental premise of the democratic system is that public opinion must be openly and frequently expressed about issues confronting society. How else can citizens make known their feelings about matters that so directly affect their lives? One constitutionally-protected means of voicing opinion is the ballot. Yet this viable instrument of democratic participation would be weakened, if not lose its whole purpose, if unqualified persons were granted the franchise or individuals marred the voting process by repeated voting in an election. For these reasons, registration systems were created.

When our country was made up of small towns and neighbors knew one another, it was hardly necessary for the registrar of elections to have an official means of checking voters whom the official knew personally. However, a different situation prevailed when the size of the electorate grew and urbanization increased. This inevitably resulted in a loss of neighborly knowledge of one's fellow citizens, and the obvious need for some method of identifying voters. The Massachusetts legislature recognized the problem as early as 1800 when it enacted a registration law, a step soon followed by other New England states. In other sections of the country, registration systems were not established until after the Civil War, but by about 1890 most states had adopted some arrangements for the systematic listing of voters, especially for the electorates in the cities (See: Joseph P. Harris, "Election Administration in the United States", Washington: Brookings Institution, 1934, p. 18).

The registration systems of the early 1900's, however, left much to be desired (See: "Modern Voter Registration Systems", National Municipal League, N.Y., 1954, partially rev. 1957). They were usually implemented periodically by precinct registrars who entered the names of voters in large cumbersome volumes, and were sometimes paid "by the name", a financial temptation bound to produce repeated abuses. Lists of registrants were padded by entering fictional names or failing to strike the names of voters who moved away or died. Because this system created inaccuracies, it was necessary to permit voters to swear to their qualifications at the polls on Election Day, thus opening another wide loophole for voting fraud.

Ingenious methods were devised to beat the system. Months before an election, political party workers rounded up persons over 21 years of age in transient and rooming house districts for registration. If these new "voters" could not be located on Election Day, their names would be voted by other people. Fictitious names were a special problem in some urban centers. Registrants found to "reside" in vacant lots, industrial buildings, or graveyards were not uncommon. In the 1868 presidential election, New York's Boss Tweed arranged for the "naturalization" of more than 50,000 ineligible aliens, all of whom not coincidentally voted for the Tweed candidate. Even as late as 1940, by which time registration abuses had been recognized as a national disgrace, Kansas City's Boss Pendergast preserved his power base with the help of over 50,000 "phantom voters."

Such obvious frauds aroused clean government and civic crusaders who insisted on registration reform. From 1927 on, the National Municipal League has advocated among other electoral reforms a permanent registration system administered by nonpartisan professionals and designed to insure updated voter lists and proper voter identification procedures. To the drive for more honest registration systems had been added the modern-day demand for change on the part of those eager to increase voting participation, especially those desiring to deepen the political involvement of disadvantaged groups--racial and ethnic minorities, women, the young and the poor. (For a more detailed account of this development, see the discussion on page 42).

Despite imperfections in the existing system, registration is practiced in all but one state (North Dakota) and a few sparsely-populated rural areas. The main test used for identification is the voter's signature. Such a system provides a suitable check list permitting no one to vote whose name does not appear on the registration list. Duplicate voting is avoided by such a procedure, and other people cannot be substituted for the registrant.

Variety of Registration Systems

There are basically two different kinds of registration systems now operating as part of the election process: periodic or permanent, depending on whether the elector must re-register at stated intervals or not. Within these classifications, registration may be personal or non-personal, depending on whether the elector may only register in person or whether the laws also provide for registration by mail.

From the standpoint of both the voter and the registrar, there are disadvantages to a periodic system of registration. For the voter, the necessity of re-registering is a nuisance; it requires time and attention to meet the deadline. In some areas where re-registration offices are open only a few days per month or only sporadically throughout the year, and where there is no provision for absentee registration, the voter who is traveling or ill may find it not only inconvenient but even impossible to register at the proper time. For the registrar, re-doing a complete registration list every few years imposes a heavier clerical, administrative and expense burden than the continuous revision of lists under a permanent system. On the other hand, some electoral procedure analysts maintain that because, under a permanent system, the name of a voter who has moved from a district or is otherwise disqualified may not be removed from the lists for several years, a periodic system is the only sure way of obtaining a "clean list", an accurate list of all voters who are currently in good standing.

In spite of such criticisms, most experts commend the efficiency and economy of a permanent registration system. It is further regarded as more convenient and thus an encouragement to voting--not an unimportant consideration in light of the voting statistics which show that millions of Americans do not take advantage of their right to join in the selection of government leaders. Furthermore, a centralized system of permanent registration, organized and run by a professional staff, is likely to be more accurate and free from fraud than a decentralized system under which precinct officers, temporarily appointed for the job at the recommendation of their political parties, undertake to register voters at frequent intervals.

Over the years the permanent system has grown in favor and actual use. By 1940, permanent registration laws had been enacted in practically all of the populous urban states outside of the south. Two decades later all but 14 states followed this system and today Arizona and South Carolina are the only states in the nation that fail to operate under a permanent registration plan of one kind or another. Interestingly, Arizona switched from a permanent to a periodic system in 1971. The Arizona lawmakers thought that the need to "wipe the slate clean" every 10 years was greater than the advantages of a permanent system. Most states have a simple one-time registration system whereby a voter registers only once. If the elector votes with the required regularity (usually at least once every two or four years) and does not change legal residence or name, there is no need to register again. There are several variations of this method. Some rural areas, as in parts of Illinois, Iowa, Kansas, Missouri, Minnesota, Nebraska and Ohio, permit voting without registration because neighbors know each other and there is no worry about fraud. North Dakota requires no registration for voting in federal or state elections, but may require it in certain municipal elections at the option of the local municipality--although the option has never been exercised. In Vermont, a permanent record in the form of a "checklist" of voters, revised at each election, is maintained.

The periodic registration rule that Arizona and South Carolina follow says that a voter must re-register in person every ten years (in South Carolina a voter registered before January 1, 1898 is considered registered for life); North Carolina and Mississippi have permanent registration systems, but are among several states that provide for re-registration at the option of local election officials. This arrangement, seemingly aimed at revising the lists periodically, appears reasonable. But it can be used as a discriminatory weapon to curb voting, as shown by the 1971 challenge made in 20 Mississippi counties where re-registration was ordered. Civil rights forces contended that the order effectively nullified the long and arduous efforts of black leaders in registering over 280,000 black Mississippians. A variation of this technique, called "reidentification of voters", has been used recently in Alabama to accomplish a similar result.

Although prospective civilian voters present themselves only once to the registration official, in 22 states (Alabama, Arkansas, Connecticut, Delaware, Florida, Georgia, Kentucky, Louisiana, Maryland, Massachusetts, Mississippi, Missouri, Nevada, New Jersey, North Carolina, Ohio, Oklahoma, Pennsylvania, Rhode Island, South Carolina, Virginia and Washington) that appearance must be made in person. Several of these states make sole exceptions for civilians temporarily residing or working outside the continental limits of the United States. (Alabama, Georgia, Massachusetts and Washington.) But even in these instances, the general rule forbids absentee registration.

The advantages of having voters present themselves are obvious: personal information on age, residence, occupation and so forth can be more accurately elicited and recorded; any question about qualifications can be cleared up immediately; and voters can be more thoroughly instructed concerning the regulations pertaining to suffrage.

Absentee Registration for Civilians and Military Personnel

It is axiomatic that the increasingly mobile American society makes necessary a set of procedures for absentee registration. Twenty-seven states now provide for general civilian absentee registration with most applying to any qualified elector. (Alaska, Arizona, California, Colorado, Hawaii, Idaho, Indiana, Iowa, Kansas, Maine, Michigan, Minnesota, Montana, Nebraska, Nevada, New Hampshire, New Mexico, New York, Oregon, South Dakota, Tennessee, Texas, Utah, Vermont, West Virginia, Wisconsin, and Wyoming. Additionally, virtually every state provides for absentee registration of some form or another for physically handicapped or disabled voters.) Virtually all of these provide that absentee registration is available only if the voter is away from county or state of residence. Tennessee and New York grant the privilege only to those electors absent because of their regular business or occupation. Wisconsin allows only electors temporarily located more than 50 miles from their legal residence to register absentee. Specific state requirements are described in Appendix I.

Members of the armed forces face special problems because of their enforced absence from their original voting site. So, all states permit absentee registration by military personnel. This same assistance is often accorded members of the Merchant Marine, civilian government employees residing overseas, and persons in religious or welfare groups accompanying or serving with the armed forces (American Red Cross, Society of Friends, U.S.O., etc.). Their spouses and dependents also are generally granted the right of absentee registration. The chart on page 107 specifies which classes of voters are included in a state's "military" voter category. One innovation boosting military absentee registration is the Federal Post Card Application (FPCA), which also relates to absentee voting. (See Chapter 4, "Can You Vote When Absent From Home?" for further details on absentee voting.) In 13 states receipt of a request for an absentee ballot via a FPCA meets the absentee registration requirement. Nine states (Arkansas, Illinois, Kansas, Missouri, New Jersey, Oklahoma, Rhode Island and Wisconsin) go even further and permit military personnel to vote without being registered. See Appendix II for specific requirements.

Movements for Registration Reform

As the winds of social change sweep various blocs in society along the path of political organization, the existing elaborate state structures for voter registration are regarded as impediments to boosting the voting strength of those groups. The panacea proposed is a national uniform registration law under the auspices of the federal government.

Reformists argue that the complicated variety of state laws, the inconvenient hours kept by many local registrars, and the often inaccessible location of registration places (as in urban centers far away from rural voters) actually discourage voting, especially among the poor and illiterate. Several proposals have been advanced in the Congress in recent years which focus on particular shortcomings recognized in the present patchwork system of state law. These proposals seek to broaden voter participation while preventing multiple voting and election fraud.

One proposal, sponsored by an impressive array of political personalities, would create a central federal registration system administered by a "Universal Voter Registration Administration" within the Bureau of the Census. Senators Kennedy, Bayh, Eagleton, Hart, Hartke, Hughes, McGovern, Magnuson, Mondale, Muskie, Pell, Ribicoff and Williams have introduced Senate Bill S. 2457, 92nd Congress, 1st Session (1971). Under this system, at any time up to 30 days prior to election voters would fill out a short, uncomplicated form obtained at their nearest post office and mail it to a central location. There the cards would be reduced to computer entries and local voting centers would be established on Election Day at convenient locations. This would make registration convenient and uncomplicated. Voting fraud would be minimized, as each voter would receive notice of his or her local voting place and appear there on Election Day where a list of those permitted to vote would be waiting. Presumably, all the voter would have to do before casting his or her ballot is to present proper identification and sign his or her name to match the signature on the mailed registration card.

This appears to be an easy, simple scheme. But it has been criticized largely on the ground of its too ambitious scope. The plan envisions the registration by mail of upwards of 100 million qualified voters. At 500 voters per polling place (about the national average, although this number varies significantly in various localities; see Chapter 3 "How Does the Voting System Work?"), no less than 200,000 polling places would be required throughout the country. Anyone with computerized billing experience can testify to the parade of administrative horrors that could follow. The human error in deciphering voters' handwriting on the postcards, the illegibility of some names, the confusion between first and last names, the problem of the voter who changes residence between registration and election, various mechanical computer errors, and other problems would all combine, some argue, to create a technological nightmare. When measured against the realization that even a minor error can mean irrevocable loss of a person's right to vote, the significance of the problem comes into sharp focus.

Several refinements of the basic federal registration plan have been introduced. Hawaii's Senator Inouye and others (Senate Bill S. 1199, 92d Congress, 1st Session (1971)) recommended a similar centralized system under which the federal government would register voters quadrenially, three weeks prior to the Presidential election. Although the bill does not specify it, such a procedure envisions registering voters door-to-door rather than by mail. This would require an enormous number of individuals to administer the system; and its efficacy in urban areas is highly questionable.

Senator Humphrey (as well as Sen. Inouye in his proposal) has suggested a procedure which would largely eliminate identification problems. A "certificate of registration", like those still issued by some states, would be given to each voter. Presentation of the certificate would be sufficient for voter-identification purposes at the polling place. This idea can be faulted, however, because it doesn't answer the problem of lost or stolen (or forged!) certificates.

Undoubtedly as the campaign for registration reform picks up steam, other more drastic variations will be offered. For example, one substitute for a federally-administered procedure is that states should continue to register voters in their customary manner, but under uniform rules and regulations promulgated by the federal government. These rules, while encouraging pre-election registration, would include a provision permitting voters who forgot or who were unable to register previously to register at the polling place when they arrive to vote on Election Day. This plan, like so many others, appears sound, but its implementation raises grave problems.

The prime purpose of a registration system is to prevent fraudulent or double voting, yet the Election-Day registration approach would not bar a voter from "registering" under two different names and addresses (perhaps at two different polling places!) and voting twice. Proponents argue that most Americans would abide by the rules and that poll watchers or challengers would be a safeguard against those voters who did not. (See Chapter 3 for a definition of these functions). Poll watchers and challengers, however, are not always familiar even with all residents of their particular voting area, so their chance of catching a double voter from a new district seems remote. While an Election Day registration system may be viable in a rural setting (note the North Dakota experience), the impersonal character of urban life probably demands a more structured design.

Although little constitutional objection can be offered to federal administration of voter registration in federal elections (See South Carolina v. Katzenbach and Oregon v. Mitchell, summarized in Appendix IV to which all of the above-described legislation applies) the central problem of these suggestions' practicality still remains. And guardians of civil liberties are bound to register an even more serious objection: the fear of violations of the right of privacy that a federally-centralized list of all citizens can generate. Federal agencies, and their state and local counterparts, could find the listing of millions of Americans an easy checklist for myriad kinds of investigations into the lives of citizens.

Certainly the present registration system can be improved. And the solutions should lie in federal laws directed at existing state systems. A federal statute mandating certain minimum state procedures, such as maintaining a fixed number of registration centers, open a specified number of hours and at times convenient for the community, appears to offer the best response to present registration inadequacies.

The Administrative Details of Registration

The state official who ordinarily assumes legal responsibility for the entire election system is the Secretary of State. Any question regarding election privileges or requirements may be directed to him or to the official registrar in a voter's local district. The Secretary usually has a multi-membered Election Board or Commission to assist him in formulating policy and supervising election practices. In the county, the registration official may be known by a variety of titles: Recorder, Clerk, Auditor or Registrar. The authority for county registration may be vested in a board such as the Board of Election Supervisors, the County Board of Registrars, the County Election Commission or the Board of Civil Authority. In smaller communities the registrar may be the municipal or town clerk or a justice of the peace. In short, there is no uniformity of title or structure in the administration of the various state systems. Usually local election officers are appointed, while generally the county and state board members are often elected for a term of several years. Most election boards and commissions are politically balanced with representatives from both major parties.

The local registrar is entrusted with the job of administering and executing the multifarious details of the registration system. The work is largely clerical, for in addition to maintaining registration lists, records are kept on personnel, voting statistics, financial accounts, and cases of election irregularities with which the election board may deal. The registrar is also responsible for ascertaining whether a particular elector fulfills the necessary qualifications to vote.

Despite the heavy emphasis on varied administrative responsibilities, or perhaps because of it, registrars are in a key position to use their office for political objectives. As noted in Chapter I's discussion of literacy tests, before the 1965 Voting Rights Act was adopted, hostile registrars in many states by various devices thwarted black voters' efforts to gain the franchise. However, the 1965 law established a mechanism for overcoming such practices by authorizing the appointment of federal registrars to supercede local registrars in places where the "automatic trigger" takes effect (see p. 18). The law empowered the Attorney General to name such federal officials for any federal, state or local election when written complaints are received from 20 or more residents in an area claiming that they have been denied the franchise on grounds of race or color. The appointments can also be made on the Attorney General's own initiative if that official certifies that discriminatory methods are utilized to interfere with the voting right guarantee of the 15th Amendment.

The federal registration technique definitely has proved a boon to expanding the franchise, as attested by this excerpt from a House of Representatives subcommittee report issued when the 1970 Voting Rights Act Amendments were being debated in Congress:

Negro registration in the five states where Federal examiners have been appointed (Alabama, Georgia, Louisiana, Mississippi, and South Carolina) has risen from approximately 29 percent to approximately 52 percent of the Negro voting-age population. This rise in nonwhite registration has been accompanied by an increase in Negro voting participation and in the number of Negro officeholders and legislators.

The sizeable rise in Negro registration, welcome though it is, does not mean the problem is ended. Roadblocks to registration of black voters are still being set in parts of the South and the recalcitrant attitude of local registrars has generated appeals for continued federal supervision. With literacy tests and similar devices outlawed, other means, both subtle and direct, are employed to stymie registration of Negroes. John Lewis, executive director of the Voter Education Project, Inc., documented the abuses in his testimony before the House Judiciary Committee on July 10, 1971:

At the point of registration, many blacks must face harrassment and intimidation from local registrars. We have received several reports of registrars closing their offices during registration campaigns, claiming they could not handle the volume of paperwork.

We have reports of registration offices having irregular hours during black registration drives--offices opening late and closing early, long lunch hours, and other delaying devices. We have encountered policies of permitting only one applicant in the registrar's office during black voter drives, while the normal policy is that more than one could enter. These and other slowdown tactics are obviously designed to discourage the weary black registrant who must endure such delays if he is to exercise his rights.

From several states, we continue to receive reports of registrars rejecting elderly blacks, obviously over 18 or 21 years of age, because they cannot document proof of age.

In several instances, we have found that registration schedules are unannounced and unavailable to black citizens. Other barriers to the ballot include locations of registration offices so as to be relatively inaccessible to black voters, hours which make it impossible for blacks to vote without leaving work and possibly losing their jobs, and offices being open for a very limited number of days per month.

The days of outright abuse and hostility from local registrars are still with us. Just this week we received a report
from a Mississippi registration worker, a part of which I
will quote. It begins:

"The County Circuit Clerk has intimidated, insulted, har-
rassed, and misinformed the Black Citizens. He has,
throughout his term, referred to Blacks as garbage, nig-
gers, and many other names that I cannot state."

The allegation continues that one black lady was told, "If
you can't say 'Yes Sir' to me, get the hell out of my damn
office."

Even this discouraging report doesn't alter the fact that the
enlarged legal protection of voting rights contained in federal
legislation and judicial decisions has fostered large-scale activity by groups interested in promoting more active use of the
franchise. Aimed primarily at increasing the participation of
previously politically alienated citizens, especially among the
poor and illiterate where the rate of registration is traditionally
lowest, various novel techniques have been devised. (Of those
citizens with 0 to 4 years of elementary education, only 38.4%
of those eligible to vote actually registered in 1970.)

The bi-racial Southern Regional Council has come up with
several ingenious and effective methods to spur registration.
Speaking tours by famous black political leaders often culminate
in a registration drive. Dances (free for registered voters),
raffles (won by the family with the most members registered),
prizes, and entertainment (half-price for registered voters)
stimulate community interest. Spot radio announcements, door-
to-door canvassing and rallies are also featured. A manual
distributed by the Voter Education Project, Inc., an affiliate of
the Council, describes in point-by-point fashion the details of
"How to Conduct a Registration Campaign". Negro student and
church groups are in the forefront of these special registration
drives as black communities increasingly involve themselves
in election contests.

Young people, drawn to the political process because 18-
year-olds now have the vote, have turned their energy and creati-
vity to the details of political participation. A student registration movement concentrating on over 300 college campuses
throughout the country has been mounted by the National Movement for the Student Vote. One group, The Youth Citizenship
Fund, focuses on large metropolitan areas. Outdoor rallies,

reportedly drawing up to 30,000 young people, have been held. Certain states which allow registration by "mobile registrars" encourage this technique by permitting registration at the rallies. A New York project, "Registration Summer", trained about 60 young interns to organize rallies and conferences in more than a dozen states. Weekend conferences specialize in instructing young leaders in local election laws and political organization.

Revision of Registration Lists

In most states the registrar has the duty to revise the registration lists, giving that official the power to cancel registrations as well as make them. The job of keeping voting lists up to date requires constant attention because of the increased mobility of the American population and the precise residence requirements imposed by the states. There are several methods by which information on voters is gathered by registration boards.

In some states, the registrar is empowered to make regular house-to-house canvasses; in others, the canvas is made by mail. Kentucky provides that in first-class cities at least 45 days before any election, two investigators appointed by the Board of Registration Commissioners conduct a house-to-house survey. Such a canvass may be requested for specific precincts by political parties. In Maryland, a canvass may be undertaken by the clerks of the Board of Registry when "any precinct is in need of a detailed check for the purpose of correcting the registration lists. . ."

In different size cities and population groups in Missouri, various provisions are made for canvasses to be conducted by mail or in person no more than 20 days before elections. Illinois' local registrars are authorized to conduct periodic canvasses of the lists, and the County Clerks mail a "Notice of Suspension of Registration" to each registered voter in counties under 500,000 who has not voted in the past four years. If the notice of suspension is not returned within 30 days with an enclosed "Application for Reinstatement of Registration", the voter's registration is cancelled. Thus the burden of proof is shifted to the voter to prove the validity of residence and registration.

Ohio's Board of Elections is empowered to conduct a check on registration 60 days prior to each general election (except in years when a general registration is held). West Virginia provides for a biennial check of the registration list if the County Court decides such a check necessary. In Louisiana, too, an annual canvass is made by the registrar, who then notifies by mail any elector whose registration is questioned. If the elector does not appear in answer to the notification, the name is finally dropped from the register.

Another method of gleaning information for the purpose of cleansing registration lists is to require reports from various state departments, health authorities, utility companies, and from the courts. In Ohio, the county health officer, probate judge and the clerk of the Court of Common Pleas file monthly reports which enable the Board of Elections to remove from the registration files names of electors who have died or who have been committed to asylums or to prison. In Illinois, the County Clerk may use information from utility companies, the post office or other sources to determine when voters move from one residence to another, and the statutes give that official the initiative in notifying electors of the procedure for transferring their registration.

Every supplier of gas, water, phone service and electricity operating in each Kentucky county is required by law to report to the County Clerk on the fifth business day of every month the names of all persons who have moved out of the county, and every city department is required to notify the election board weekly of anyone who has moved. The Clerk may, on the basis of reliable information, transfer the registration records from one precinct to another or otherwise change the registration, but notification to the voter of the revision of the record is required. The Clerk is also empowered to clear the registration lists of the names of all those who have been committed for insanity or crime or who have moved away. Maryland also provides for official notice from the appropriate agencies of all electors who are deceased, or who have been convicted or institutionalized. In Michigan, the Clerk is required to check with the register of vital statistics at least once a month and is empowered to cancel all registrations of electors who have died.

Other excellent sources of information are the annual surveys conducted in various states. In Maine the assessors make an annual check each spring, visiting every building in every city and town, and listing all owners and occupants with information on age, name, and occupation; this compilation provides invaluable information for revision of registration lists. A similar procedure is followed in Massachusetts where an annual register of all persons is compiled by the local registrars. Voters not included in this register are notified in June, and if they present

43

adequate evidence of the right to be reinstated on the registration list, the name is added.

One of the best ways to check on a voter's continued existence as registered is the voting record. Almost all of the states, 43 to be exact, set up definite time intervals for eliminating non-voters from registration lists. In such states the registration officials check the records after each election and cancel registrants who have not voted within recent years; such action is not necessary, of course, in a periodic system (which only Arizona and South Carolina follows), but is extremely important in a permanent one. The following summary will give an indication of the time spans established by different states:

Registration cancelled for failure to vote every 4 years: Alaska; Arkansas; Delaware; Illinois; Iowa; Louisiana (2 years in Orleans parish); Minnesota; Missouri (4 years in some counties, 2 years in others); Nebraska; New Jersey; South Dakota; Tennessee; Utah; Virginia (as of December 31, 1974); West Virginia.

Registration cancelled for failure to vote every 2 years: Arizona; California; Colorado; Florida; Hawaii; Indiana; Kansas; Kentucky; Louisiana (in Orleans parish); Massachusetts; Michigan; Missouri (two years in some counties, four years in others); Montana; Nevada; New Hamshire; New Mexico; New York; Ohio; Oklahoma; Oregon; Pennsylvania; Washington (30 months); Wisconsin; and Wyoming.

Other State Requirements

Georgia and Texas (3 years); Maryland and Rhode Island (5 years); Idaho (8 years); North Carolina (6 years in counties with over 10,000 population).

Times for Registration

The official registration periods vary considerably. In a large number of states, the days and hours when a voter may register closes several weeks before each election to enable the registrars to compile final lists of voters and distribute these official lists to party and poll officials. The registrars are required by law to announce the times for registration in local newspapers and in official notices. Wide publicity is important to ensure that no elector is prevented from registering because of uncertainty or ignorance about the proper time for registration.

In most permanent registration systems, the office of the registrar is open during regular business hours throughout the year except for the period immediately preceding the election; under South Carolina's periodic registration law the registrar's office is open only on stated days. Appendix I describes registration details on a state-by-state basis, but the voter is advised to check registration hours with his local registration board.

Late Registration

Registration laws are somewhat more flexible than the precise description of hours and days for regular registration would suggest. Many states take special account of the voter who has been ill, or who qualifies to register (by becoming 18, fulfilling the residence requirement, or returning from military service) after the official registration deadline. The interpretation of most registration rules is decidedly in the voter's favor, even to the point of allowing some voters to produce evidence of their qualifications at the polls and to be duly registered on Election Day. As the state codes reveal many exceptions to the regular registration procedure, the voter is urged to consult the laws for guidance.

The Voter's Registration Requirements

The actual registration procedure is in most states quite simple, and although variations exist from state to state, it is possible to describe the usual steps. When an elector goes to the office of the registrar, he or she is asked to answer under oath certain questions about residence, age, citizenship, and all of the other qualifications. Since such data will thereafter identify the person at the polls, the voter must be very careful to answer correctly and to sign his or her name as they ordinarily do. In most states, the full name is required, or at least the middle initial if the middle name is not used. Since the signature is the key to the identification of the voter, it is very important that the signing be done in the usual manner, as often a signature is disallowed on a nominating petition or in signing at the polls because it does not compare exactly with the original signature on the registration record. If an elector is a naturalized citizen, he or she should take with them to the registration place their "Certificate of Naturalization" (original or certified copy) which attests to naturalization. If the registrant has lost the official paper, he or she should obtain a new certificate from the Immigration and Naturalization Service. Alternatively, naturalized citizens may complete a Form N-585 at their local INS office where, for a small fee, the INS will forward the desired verification to the local registrar. The INS will also, upon written request of the registrar, verify directly the applicant's citizenship status.

Based on a sampling of many states, the problems of voter-identification seem to have been largely eliminated through the use of various identification or registration certificates. South Carolina, for example, issues a "Certificate" which attests to the fact that a voter is registered. The certificate includes certain identifying information as to eye and hair color, etc. Florida issues a "Registration Identification Card" (called simply an "Identification Card" in Oklahoma). Alabama is one of several states which issues a "Certificate of Registration" to each voter when he or she registers.

Most states which provide a voter some extrinsic proof of registration also have procedures for replacing a lost or stolen certificate or identification card. The increase in absentee registration provisions, however, as well as the administrative problems of any regular registration identification system have decreased the importance of such special identification procedures. The voter's signature still remains the most useful and widespread source of identification.

Challenge of Registrants

Just as there are political party representatives whose job it is to challenge voters at the polls, so party challengers are usually present at any public registration or revision session for the purpose of questioning registration applicants. Grounds for such challenge are clearly stated in the state codes, usually insufficient residence or failure to meet other required qualifications. The challenge is declared to the official election board or registrar as a person applies to register, or a challenge may be filed in writing in advance of the public session. The registering authority acknowledges the challenge, questions the applicant under oath as to any retort to the challenge, and then passes on the validity of the application or the challenge. When a voter is refused the right to register, he or she may seek recourse to a higher election authority or, failing of success with the administrative branch, may take a final appeal to the courts. Frequently such a challenge may be only a party maneuver to harrass registrants of the opposition party, but more often it serves constructively as a check on attempts by unqualified persons to gain access to the ballot.

Transfer of Registration

Under most state requirements, the elector is obliged to notify the registrar when there is a change of residence or party affiliation. In some states, a voter is required to re-register under these circumstances, but in most states notification of the appropriate officials suffices. Whenever an elector moves from one precinct to another or from county to county within a state, he or she is usually required to notify the registration authorities of the new address and to request the cancellation of the previous registration. If the voter moves during the time when registration is closed, certain states permit the person to vote in the former precinct for one election immediately following the change of residence, but expect a change of registration as soon as possible. In some cases, however, the elector may not vote in the old precinct and may not register in the new district until he or she has lived there for the legally prescribed length of time.

An elector whose name is changed either by marriage or through a court order usually is directed to notify the registration officials so that they may revise their records. In some states a new registration is required; in others the voter may simply notify the authorities in person or by mail of the change of name, and the registration card will be corrected without complete re-registration. And in certain instances, especially in the case of a woman who has married, the name change may be effected when she goes to the polls on Election Day.

In all but a few of the fifty states, an elector must be enrolled as a member of a political party before he or she may participate in the primary election by which party candidates are nominated.* However, enrollment in an American political party does not bind the registrant too tightly. Enrollment is not an official act of joining the party, a promise to pay dues, or in fact even to participate actively in party activities. Enrollment is simply a declaration by the voter when registering that he or

---

* Two states, Alaska and Washington, permit registered voters to vote in the primary of more than one political party.

she is a member of a certain party. In some states, if a voter's affiliation is challenged at the polls by members of the party with which affiliation is claimed, the person must swear under oath that he or she supported the nominees of that party in previous elections and intends to back them in the next general election. In other words, party affiliation in the United States is a matter of voter intention rather than an officially-executed membership.

In nearly every state, an elector is prevented by law from transferring from one party to another within at least one month and usually for several months before the forthcoming primary. The purpose of such a regulation is to prevent members of one party from temporarily shifting their affiliation in order to participate in the opposition party's nominations. The practice, known as "raiding", is a means by which members of one party might participate in the primary of their opponents in order to swell the vote for the weakest opposition candidate; if the "raid" is successful, competition is reduced for the raiders' own candidate in the general election. The elaborate arrangements in most states for changing party affiliation and the time restrictions on voting after an affiliation change strongly deter most voters from attempting a shift for other than honest purposes--that is, a change of party loyalty made in good faith.

However, some states view such a cross-over as desireable rather than detrimental (see Chapter 3, "How Does the Voting System Work?", section on Primary Elections, for details). As the American electorate has shown a more independent streak in recent elections, in those states numbers of voters have crossed over to another party's primaries to express support for candidates of their liking.

Chapter 3

HOW DOES THE VOTING SYSTEM WORK?

Democratic institutions are rarely revered for their sense of orderliness and simplicity. As people and structure intertwine, the workings of government necessarily are complex and frequently vexatious. Indeed, if the average voter reviewed the intricate network of laws which form the framework of the voting process, he or she would not only be overwhelmed but amazed that the process works at all. (But such consternation is a small price to pay for democracy's highest prize, the choosing of government's leaders by the people themselves.)

Despite the growth of federal power in the electoral area, the states still possess the authority to supervise the technical, voluminous aspects of voting. The state codes, which vary in some respects and can run as long as several hundred pages, specify myriad administrative details, including the defining of election personnel, their duties and the exact procedures which they and the voter must follow if the election is to be "legal".

The "rule of law" in a democratic society requires that attention be paid to minute detail, so the statutory voting laws which are such an integral part of the voting process must be examined carefully to understand the nature of the franchise in the United States. The important role of the election official should be scrutinized before looking at the procedural requirements governing the voter.

Administrative Responsibility

The administration of elections falls mainly within the governmental jurisdiction of each state. More specifically, the Secretary of State or a state official of similar rank is responsible. Power is delegated by the government official to election boards or their counterparts at the county level, and then to the countless ward and precinct officials or election judges who conduct the actual polling in the neighborhoods. Many procedures connected with the polling are regularized throughout the state: registration requirements, polling hours and the methods for casting and tallying ballots are usually standard. (The issue of polling hours has reached proportions of national concern because of the three-hour difference between east and west coast time zones. With the advent of television the charge has been made that candidates and parties can influence voters on the west coast who have not yet gone to the polls by reporting election results and trends from the eastern parts of the country.) Other details are more likely to vary from place to place within a state. Such matters as the rearrangement of election districts to accommodate population changes, whether to use paper ballots or voting machines and the arrangements for election supplies and polling locations are within the province of local officials.

Each polling place is run by at least two election judges or supervisors who usually belong to different political parties--in all states where there are two viable parties to provide such representatives. In some states these judges must be of "upright character," and usually are also required to take an oath that they will properly and honestly perform their duties. For obvious reasons, such judges may not themselves be candidates for office, nor may they be actively engaged in any candidate's campaign. In polling districts with large numbers of voters, several election clerks may be appointed. Named on a non-partisan basis, the clerks assist the judges with the various jobs of verifying and checking off the voter's name in the registration book, handing out the ballot, making certain that the procedure for marking a ballot or using a voting machine is understood, assisting the physically disabled or blind voter and counting and reporting the final results after the polls close.

These administrative assignments are not tackled in a haphazard way. With an eye toward professionalizing the function of election officials and obtaining their opinions on improvements in the broad field of election administration, a number of states conduct training schools and seminars for these officials. Before every primary and biennial general election, Michigan's Director of Elections arranges a series of training sessions for county clerks and election inspectors or their representatives. In Georgia the Secretary of State and the State Election Board hold similar training conferences and also distribute election information to local registrars. Two state-wide conferences are held by Connecticut's Secretary of State with town clerks and registrars to discuss election laws. A parallel procedure is followed in Oklahoma where the Secretaries of the County election boards attend election law study conferences conducted under the auspices of the State Election Board.

In addition to the official poll workers paid by the state or political subdivision, every voting place usually has several poll watchers, challengers and party checkers on the scene. State laws provide for their appointment and duties, but these people cannot be considered "officials". They are not entitled to count ballots or participate in the other official business of the polls. Sitting at a table separate from the official poll workers, the watchers and challengers are present to serve their political parties rather than the state. They defend their party's interests by challenging any voter whom they believe to be legally unqualified, and by questioning any election practice they regard as prejudicial to their party.

Several such representatives may serve at each poll, and are entitled to witness all election transactions throughout the day until all ballots have been counted and recorded. They are specificially prohibited from any type of electioneering, and of course may not interfere with any individual who is involved in the act of voting. They are mainly watchdogs, alert to any threat to partisan interests; and their partisan alertness inevitably contributes to the public interest. For the poll watchers watch each other, an excellent guarantee against electoral chicanery.

The party checkers also play a more affirmative role at the polls which frequently can affect the outcome of the election. They keep a running count on party members as they vote. If, toward the end of the polling hours, the list shows that known party supporters have not voted, they are rounded up by partisan workers and urged to go to the polls.

The Details of Voting

In the hurly-burly of election contests, where the rich rewards of party and personal power are at stake, candidates and parties are keenly aware of the need to challenge voters who may not be qualified to vote (especially if they have registered in a different party!).

Generally the state election codes describe the exact procedure for the challenge of voters, beginning with the grounds on which a challenge may be brought down to the specific questions which the voter must answer in refuting the challenge. Challengers may question an individual's right to vote on a number of counts--betting on the election results, attempting to vote a second time or simply voting under an improper registration.

When a voter is challenged for these or other reasons, the

ARNEGIE LIBRARY

LIVINGSTONE COLLEGE

SALISBURY, N. C. 28144

decision on the validity of the voter's qualification most often is made by the presiding election officials. Missouri's election judges, for example, are empowered to reject the vote of a voter found to be disqualified. The law provides, however, that no person's vote may be rejected "except upon the testimony of two credible witnesses." In Oregon and several other states, any election board clerk or any elector has the right to challenge a voter whom he or she suspects to be unqualified. The challenged voter can vote if a declaration of qualification is made under oath, but in such a case the poll book contains the notation "challenged and sworn" and the ballot is specially marked so that it can be discounted if the challenge is finally upheld. This type of procedure is necessary because usually there is not adequate time during polling hours to allow for the appeal and reinstatement of a challenged voter. If some means is not provided for allowing such a person to vote provisionally, the elector's vote may be unjustifiably lost.

Timeliness is obviously a key element in pressing a challenge and the procedures noted above concern Election Day challenges authorized in 49 states. Only Vermont does not provide for such a procedure. The questioning of voters' qualifications can also take place before Election Day. Most states have procedures allowing challenges to be made to a voter's registration in advance of the election. (See page 46).

Complete registration lists, including both regular and absentee voters, are ordinarily sent by the election boards to the political parties and candidates before each election. If a party contests a name on this official list, the challenge may be heard and judged by the election board several weeks before the election. The elector then has adequate time to appeal to the county registrar, the county court, or another legally-designated appeal board for reversal of an adverse decision. In New Mexico, for example, the county chairman of each political party receives advance lists of the registered voters, and during the 42 days before an election the chairman may petition for the admission of a party member or challenge the registration of members of the opposition. Similarly in Maryland, official registration lists are available, for a nominal fee, to anyone who applies. Any person may file an objection to another registered voter with the Board of Supervisors, so long as the complaint is filed several months before the election. The Board of Registry sits to hear objections and is authorized to decide all cases immediately after the hearing; but the challenged voter may appeal a negative decision to the county or city courts.

The Massachusetts law provides that challenges against city voters must be filed at least 14 days before an election; remonstrances against town electors must be made at least 4 days ahead. After investigating the challenge, the registrar hears the case and then decides whether the name shall be retained or struck from the register. In Hawaii, challenges which must be specified in writing are sent to the election clerk; the election official notifies the party of the questioned voter so that a defense can be arranged. In Maine, the voter is allowed to defend himself; the law requires that a challenged voter must be notified by the clerk so that a personal appearance may be made before the registration board.

Most challenge procedures serve a constructive end by checking on attempts by unqualified persons to gain access to the ballot. But it is not uncommon for political parties to use challenges as a maneuver designed to harrass registrants of the opposition party. The following account of a 1968 primary election battle in New Haven, Conn. illuminates the problem clearly. Control of the Democratic Party apparatus wielded by the chairman of the Democratic Town Committee, was opposed by a group of liberal Democrats who attempted to organize their electoral strength at the polls. Local Democratic polling officials initiated a number of challenges, which were later rejected. As the insurgent candidate lost by 18 votes, and 20 of his supporters were barred by the faulty challenges, the badgering technique was successful. And there was no recourse in the law. Since Connecticut election law only provides for a "recount" where there is evidence of misuse of the challenge power, the losing candidate was without a remedy because his supporters did not cast their ballots. These events did, however, prompt the Yale Law Journal to advocate "A Model Voter Challenge Statute" which provides for accepting the votes of challenged voters on Election Day subject to subsequent invalidation. Hopefully, such a statute may someday replace the often ineffectual laws now operating in many states.

This random sample of various challenge and appeal procedures describes most of the kinds of checks employed by the states, and some of the problems they raise. Although the challenge is still an important safeguard against fraudulent registration and voting, the formalization and improvement of registration systems make this aspect of the voting process less significant than it once was.

The site where election ballots are cast is one which is convenient for the voters. Local election officials entrusted with the choice of locations for polling places usually select a school or other public building. In order to insulate voters from pressure, intimidation, or other undue influences, election codes contain a number of prohibitions relating to activity at the polling place. The major restriction, common to all states, is that polls not be located in a place where alcoholic beverages are sold, or in a location which is not easily accessible to all electors. Election Day regulations also prohibit crowds from milling around the polls, and from loitering within a certain distance (usually one hundred feet) of the polling place. This protection extends to the prohibition of the distribution of campaign literature within a prescribed distance of the polls, a safeguard which so far the courts have said does not infringe constitutional standards.

A 1970 Tennessee case, Piper v. Swan, challenging on First Amendment grounds a state law prohibiting circulation of campaign literature on the same floor of a building where the "election is in progress" or within 100 feet of the polls, was dismissed by a Federal District Court and the Supreme Court declined to review the appeal. The lower federal court opinion noted the Supreme Court's implication, in its 1966 Mills v. Alabama decision, that the states have broad authority to "regulate conduct in and around the polls in order to maintain peace, order and decorum there."

The barrier to Election Day campaigning at the polling site does not affect other forms of public expression. Party representatives may appeal to voters and hand out literature at distances removed from the immediate polling site. Sound trucks may tour the community with campaign messages and radio and TV spot announcements are aired. Indeed, the Mills decision noted above invalidated an Alabama law which penalized newspapers for publishing Election Day editorials about candidates.

The maintenance of decorum at the polling premises is essential for the serious business that takes place there--making the democratic system function. So election officials are usually authorized to act as temporary sheriffs with the right to imprison any troublemaker (after he or she has voted) for a period of 24 hours; this temporarily-assumed police power is often reinforced by the presence of the local sheriff or a policeman assigned to the polls. Rarely do officials exercise these powers, but just the fact that they have such authority is a further assurance that the balloting will be orderly and uninterrupted.

54

Polling hours differ in each state. In 18 states, Election Day is a legal holiday. Election codes in 30 states say that each citizen is entitled to a certain amount of released time from employment for the purpose of voting; in a few states, the voter is legally allowed up to four hours off with no deduction in pay or other penalty for the time missed, but the more usual provision allows two or three hours. Any employer who does not honor this time-off provision (provided the employee has made arrangements with the employer prior to Election Day) is liable to fine or imprisonment.

As a shield against overcrowding the polling place, state laws also regulate the maximum number of names allowed on any one voting list. These figures vary with the type of ballot used (machine or paper). More than 1,000 voters are rarely placed on any voting list, and those states that do permit a high number invariably vote by machines, thereby ensuring a fast vote and accurate count.

The special importance attached to the voter on Election Day is suggested by other provisions of the codes. In most states, an elector on the way to the polls is immune from arrest except for such crimes as breach of the peace, treason or felony. Voters are also exempt from military duty on Election Day except in time of war or in case of a public emergency.

Once the voter moves inside a polling place, every effort is made to continue an orderly and efficient voting procedure. Voters must follow the prescribed routine, such as taking their turn in line and keeping a certain distance away from the actual balloting booths so that the voter in the booth enjoys privacy. After giving his or her name to the election clerk, who says the name clearly and distinctly for the benefit of the challengers or watchers, the voter signs the registration book or record (in some states a registration certificate or other identification or receipt may be required). The elector then casts the ballot in the prescribed manner, and leaves the polls promptly after depositing the ballot in the appropriate box or pulling the lever on the voting machine.

Most state codes feature regulations intended to expedite balloting; for example, voters are usually legally limited to two or three minutes' time in the voting booth. In all states, if a voter spoils the first ballot, by marking it incorrectly or spilling ink on or otherwise defacing it, a second ballot is provided; some states even allow a third ballot in such circumstances. This provision, of course, applies only where paper ballots are used. In what appears to be a sensible precaution, Oregon further provides that if an elector spoils three ballots, this is evidence that assistance is needed, and help is provided by two election board clerks.

In view of the wide-spread use of voting machines in today's elections, the problem of paper ballots is not a large one. Since 1892, when voting machines were first used in Lockport, New York, many states have incorporated them into the election process. By 1972, 48 states (all but Idaho and Utah) utilized machines in at least some election precincts. Eight states (Connecticut, Delaware, Hawaii, Kentucky, Louisiana, New Mexico, New York and Rhode Island) use machines exclusively, while another (Alabama) votes 80% by machine, 20% by paper ballot. Election machines are not perfect. There frequently are reports of breakdowns in the midst of voting and difficulties arise when no alternative means for voting is available. But these mechanical deficiencies, which can be corrected, are offset by the efficiency and accuracy of machine tabulations of votes, especially in areas where the vote is large.

In the search for honest, clean elections, the states have had to face up to the realistic problem of assisting voters who are physically disabled, blind or illiterate. As Joseph P. Harris noted in his book, "Election Administration" (page 227), such assistance was formerly "one of the principal sources of election manipulation." The state codes, therefore, emphasize strict regulations designed to aid voters, with several essential factors stressed.

Obviously, the first question is to establish who should be assisted; then, to specify who is to give the help, an election official or a friend selected by the voter; and finally, to describe what kind of aid may be given. The primary concern, of course, is that the voter's privacy of decision and secrecy of vote not be needlessly jeopardized because of his or her infirmity; or, to be more exact, that a voter's disability not create a situation where the electoral decision and actual casting of the vote is subject to coercion or pressure. No assisted voter can be entirely independent, so the problem is intrinsically insoluble. However, the election laws contain a variety of provisions designed to minimize the difficulty.

Who qualifies for assistance as a physically disabled elector? Some states deny help at the polls unless such disability was noted on the original registration. Other states, however, consider it sufficient if the voter's disability is "apparent" to the registrar. In some cases, simply the elector's statement that help is needed suffices to obtain aid. Taking these variations into account, usually blindness, inability to use one's hands, or any other physical ailment which prevents an elector from reading or marking his ballot is considered disability warranting assistance. In several states a person may also request help in marking the ballot if the individual's religious beliefs prohibit this physical act. Certain states specifically, and all states implicitly, rule out intoxication as a justifiable reason for assistance.

There is always danger, of course, that the person who assists a voter may either unduly influence the voter or deliberately not mark the ballot as the voter directs. To prevent the possibility of such fraudulent attempts, many state laws provide that assistance to a disabled voter may only be given by the officials at the polling place, and that the elector shall be accompanied to the booth and assisted by not one but two election judges who must represent different political parties. In some states, the voter can select the officials to provide the help.

In contrast to the states which provide only for official help to the incapacitated voter, Nevada says that such a voter may designate any non-official elector to give the aid. However, there is a condition, the assisting individual may only help "at the discretion of the election board"--a protection against a concerted attempt to influence the votes of a sizable number of dependent voters. This same type of restriction is imposed in states where the voter can choose his or her helpmate from the lists of election officials or qualified voters.

The state codes contain many other special qualifications when assistance is allowed. In Minnesota, for example, the voter may choose another qualified elector to help, but that person must not assist more than three voters at one election. If a voter cannot understand English, the election officials may select two persons to serve as interpreters; but again only if they come from two different political parties. In North Carolina's general election, any voter is entitled to request help from a "near relative" of his or her choice. The relative may go with the voter into the booth and render such help as is needed; in the case of a physically disabled person, help may be received from a relative or from the registrar or one of the election judges.

An interesting variation in North Carolina's law is the section which permits voting under oath by aged or disabled persons outside of the voting enclosure, either "in the vehicle conveying such person to the voting place or in the immediate proximity of the voting place." Blind people usually are not limited to help only from election officials. Almost without exception, a blind voter is free to choose a member of the family or another qualified elector from the election district to furnish assistance.

The state laws vary also about the kinds of assistance which can be given a disabled, blind, or illiterate voter. The common procedure is for the election judges to accompany the voter into the booth and mark the ballot as directed. In Maryland, however, the voter's independence could be weakened by the requirement that the ballot choices be dictated to the relative or election officials who provide help, even though the law says the only assistance the election judges may give "is to mark the ballot or operate the voting machine, as the voter shall direct, without prompting or suggestion from them."

In Kentucky, meticulous care is taken to insure an illiterate voter's freedom from coercion and to guarantee the right to mark the ballot personally. The voter tells the clerk the party and candidate of his or her choice, and in the presence of election judges, the sheriff, the challengers and the voter, the clerk puts a pencil dot in the proper place. The voter then goes to the booth and marks the ballot. Voting secrecy is sacrificed to assure that the choice is the voter's, the guiding principle in all voting assistance laws.

During the election campaign the electorate is informed about slates of candidates and referenda issues on the ballot by numerous techniques. Political parties, independent committees, and the candidates themselves send a flood of mailings to the voters' homes. Newspaper advertisements and radio-TV spots also promote the candidates and their political party. Public rallies are held. News coverage and editorial comment in the media augment this information process.

All this would seem enough to make the elector familiar with the ballot he or she obtains at the polling booth, yet this is not always the case. So, many states send sample ballots to electors several days before the election. This enables the voters to acquaint themselves with the names and issues on the ballot and facilitates voting at the polls. Nothing prevents the voter from taking the sample ballot or any other memorandum into the booth, a definite help when multiple offices and issues are to be decided.

There are many variations among state ballots as to color, size and arrangement of offices and candidates. But there is one common characteristic, the use of the Australian ballot. This is an official ballot printed under the direction of public officials and at public expense and containing only the names of candidates who are nominated according to legally established procedures. Strange as it may seem for a democracy which loudly proclaims democratic election procedures among its most laudable virtues, the Australian ballot is a relatively recent development in American elections. Kentucky was the first state to adopt the ballot for limited use in 1888, but it was not until the late 1920's that all states accepted the idea of an official written ballot for all elections. Although written ballots were used widely prior to the 20th century, they were usually furnished by the political parties and seldom uniform.

Even though the states invariably employ the Australian ballot, there are a wide variety of differences in the official ballot. Some states list candidates for national and state offices on separate ballots; some use one long ballot which includes all national and state candidates. Diverse colored paper mark the different levels of government offices listed on Minnesota's ballots. In Wyoming, Massachusetts, California, Florida, Indiana, Maine, Maryland, New Hampshire, Oklahoma, Rhode Island, Tennessee, and South Dakota, different colors distinguish the primary ballots of the Democratic and Republican parties. In Georgia, different colors may be used if the political parties so agree. Interestingly, Washington provides that every primary ballot must be uniform in color. Montana, an "open primary" state (see below), features an unusual ballot procedure which is also followed in Utah and Wisconsin. Each elector receives a ballot comprised of tickets representing all parties fastened to the top. The elector enters the booth, detaches the preferred ticket, marks the choices and deposits the ticket in a box. The unused tickets are then placed in a separate box.

The actual form and arrangement of names on the ballots are not the same in all states. The two commonly-used groupings are the office-type (or Massachusetts) and party-column (or Indiana) ballot. The office-type ballot, used in 19 states, lists the candidates' names together under the office for which they are running, with a party designation beside each name. In the party-column plan, each party's candidates are printed in separate columns with the name of the office for which they are contending listed beside the name. The party-column ballot, now in effect in 31 states, enables a voter automatically to cast a straight party ticket for all candidates by marking a single "X" in the box or circle at the top of the column. The office-type ballot, however, requires the voter to mark the individual choice for each political office; even though the voter may vote only for the candidates of a single party. The decision represents a conscious choice about each candidate rather than the casting of a blanket party vote. The office-type ballot is generally regarded as superior to the party-column system even though the office-type ballot encourages (or at least does not discourage) cross-party voting which some students of American politics see as further weakening party discipline in the two major parties.

Any debate over which kind of official ballot should be presented to the elector would not be complete without noting that virtually all states' election codes contain provisions for write-in candidates in general elections. This is not followed by all states in primary elections where write-ins may be barred on the assumption that primaries are unrestricted and any candidate may seek a spot on the ballot.

Another interesting aspect of the ballot, one over which political chieftains continually jockey, relates to the placement of candidates' names. The "top spot" is most desirable because it immediately catches the voter's eye. Common sense and fairness would seem to dictate placing the names in random order. But this is not always the case, and as another illustration of the endless variety of state voting provisions, one must examine what the codes provide.

Many states (of which Missouri and Wisconsin are examples) give the top of the ballot to the party which polled the most votes at a preceding general election (usually for that party's gubernatorial candidate). Other codes place the decision in the hands of the government election board or official, such as Illinois' practice where the political parties are placed in the order certified by the state electoral board. In Idaho, the Secretary of State may initially place names on the ballot, but a "rotation" system is mandated for the final selection.

Under a "rotation" system, different candidates' names (or the different parties in a party-column ballot) are placed in rotating order on each group of ballots printed. The system does not necessarily assure ballot uniformity among all voting precincts within the state. Montana's rotation system, for example, provides for an initial alphabetical ordering. No problem crops up if only two candidates contest for a particular office. Only two sets of ballots will be printed with the top spot shared equally. But a different situation prevails when more than the two major party candidates appear on the ballot. Demonstrating a common variation which can affect a minority party's vote, the candidates of the two "major parties" (defined as the major vote-getters in previous elections) must appear on the ballot "before and above candidates of minor parties and independent candidates." The major party candidates "rotate" the top-spot which, by law, effectively denies to minor party or independent office-seekers the prominent visibility which any new political body needs.

New Jersey exemplifies still another alternative. In that state's office-type ballot, each county clerk draws lots to determine the order of the political parties on the ballot. This system is similar to the rotation method as the ordering of the candidates (or the parties) by chance selection may well differ from county to county.

Another detail involved in preparation of the ballot, albeit a politically sensitive one, concerns the number of times a candidate may appear on the ballot for a single office. Some states, for example, Montana and New Jersey, prohibit a candidate's name from appearing more than once. A few states, such as California and New York, permit such a practice. This explains in part why in New York State candidates vie for the valuable endorsement of the Liberal and Conservative parties. However, the New York experience is unique as most other states do not have an established multiple party structure.

Preserving the sanctity of the ballot, the keystone of the whole voting process, is an obvious need, and with the now widespread use of voting machines abuses can be limited. However, to protect the integrity of the vote in states which still use paper ballots, precaution must be taken to ensure that the ballot the voter places in the ballot box is the one that he or she marked. All states are aware of such old-time election practices as the "endless chain ballot" which grew up in the early days of American elections. A corrupt politician would stand outside the polls and give an already market ballot to a bribed voter who would take it into the polling place, substitute it for the fresh ballot given by the poll officials, and bring the unmarked ballot out to the vote buyer who could repeat the process time and again. The first link in such a chain was the acquisition of an official but unmarked ballot at the beginning of the polling day.

To combat this and other chicanery, most paper-ballot states adhere to careful measures to ensure that packages of ballots are sealed until they are delivered to the polling place. In some cases the precinct official must personally procure the ballots from a central distribution point and take them to the poll. A number of states use a numbering system for ballots as a further protection. When the voter enters the polls and signs the poll list, the name is registered beside a number which corresponds to the number on the stub of the ballot handed to the voter. After the ballot is marked, the elector hands the folded ballot to the election official who rechecks the number against the poll list. Then the official usually tears the numbered stub from the ballot and deposits it in a separate box. Such a procedure ensures that the voter has marked his or her own ballot, but does not threaten the secrecy of the ballot since the identifying number is removed with the stub.

Primary Elections

An elementary principle of the election process is the democratic selection of candidates for political office, a selection which weakens the power of party bosses and machines to hand pick their own candidates. If popular elections are to succeed, a preliminary--or primary--election in which party nominees battle each other for their party's nomination for particular offices is essential. The primaries also frequently sharpen the campaign issues and can (but not always) be a mechanism for making the party more responsive to the public's wishes. (The discussion below concerns primary elections for state office. Preferential primaries are held in these 22 states to select delegates to the national party conventions which choose presidential candidates: Arkansas, California, Florida, Illinois, Indiana, Maryland, Massachusetts, Nebraska, New Hampshire, New Jersey, New Mexico, New York, North Carolina, Ohio, Oklahoma, Oregon, Pennsylvania, Rhode Island, South Dakota, Tennessee, West Virginia, Wisconsin.)

Before the widespread growth of primary elections, political leaders chose the party's standard bearers for the public at party "caucuses" or "conventions". Candidate selections were often dictated by political machines whose commanders met in "smoke-filled rooms" to make their deals. The decisions of these men (few women reached the top of the political ladder) were usually final. The bosses' tight control of the party apparatus and their picking of the caucus or convention delegates insured support for their nominees.

Although state primary elections have had a moderating effect on the practices of hitherto unchallenged party chiefs, they have not entirely purified the selection process. Primaries still permit retention of the worst features of the old system. Candidates are sometimes "endorsed" by the state central committee, thus tying the nominee to the party leadership by assuring a working organization (and sometimes party funds). Four states, Colorado, Connecticut, Massachusetts and Utah, still hold pre-primary conventions, thus strengthening the possibility of abuse.

Primaries nominate candidates for all levels of government and exist in some form in every state. The time of the state primaries vary from March to September, and the voter should check with local election officials to ascertain when and where the primary will be held in his or her state. In a few states the major party primaries are held in separate places. And in some others, such as Rhode Island and Connecticut, Republican and Democratic primaries are held at different times, sometimes as much as a week apart.

As primaries are the device through which party members express their preferences among candidates for the person whom they will support in the general election, they are usually closed to all but party members. Nine states (Alaska, Michigan, Minnesota, Montana, North Dakota, Utah, Vermont, Washington, and Wisconsin), however, hold "open primaries" where an elector may vote in any primary, regardless of party affiliation. This offers the voter greater flexibility. However, in every state but Alaska and Washington, the usual practice is to restrict the voter to casting a ballot in the primary of only one political party. And most states impose fairly rigid requirements for changing party affiliation, which discourages temporary or irresponsible shifting from one party to another. Rhode Island, for example, provides that no person shall be entitled to vote in a party primary if within 26 months he or she has voted in a primary as a member of another political party, or has signed the final nomination paper of any independent candidate.

In "open primary" states, the voter declares party affiliation, and then according to the variations in state laws, may either be given only the ballot for that party; or a single ballot on which the elector can vote only for the candidates of a single party (Idaho, Minnesota, and North Dakota); or several ballots from which one is to be used and others discarded (Michigan, Montana, Utah and Wisconsin). In Alaska and Washington, the voter may vote for people in different parties for different offices.

In several states, chiefly in the South, the election codes provide for a second or run-off primary when no candidate receives a majority of the votes cast in the first primary. Florida law calls for a run-off to be held five weeks before the general election, and Tennessee and Louisiana provide for such a primary within three and four weeks after the first primary. When the South was a one-party region, the winner of the Democratic Party run-off was virtually guaranteed victory in the general election. With the growth of the Republican Party as a viable political force in the South, however, in several states the Democratic run-off victor may face another challenge in the general elections.

The drive for open primaries is not waning and presumably will accelerate as the American electorate registers a deeper concern about issues rather than party regularity. Voters have shown increasing irritation with the power wielded by party leaders in the selection of presidential nominees, and demands are burgeoning for open state primaries (or a national presidential primary) in which the people can indicate which presidential candidate they prefer to carry the party's banner.

This revisionist mood is part of the insistence on general political party reform, which struck at the roots of the Democratic party in the back wash of the heavy dissatisfaction with the delegate selection process at the 1968 Democratic National Convention in Chicago. The unrest forced the creation of "A Party Commission on Party Structure and Delegate Selection", headed by Senator George McGovern of South Dakota. The McGovern Report, officially titled "Mandate for Reform", laid down new guidelines which already have achieved some reforms.

Criticisms of the prevailing system were based in large measure on restrictive state laws or practices which effectively denied representation at the national party convention to party dissidents or reformists who opposed the often firmly entrenched state or county political committees. These restrictive practices included the selection of delegates almost a year before the convention (thus effectively precluding representatives of newly emerging party wings), and the imposition of financial or other burdens on prospective delegates which limited delegate selection to the wealthy few who could afford to attend. The result was a number of glaring inequities. For example, blacks comprised only 5% of the voting delegates in 1968 while supplying about 20% of the Democratic vote in that year. Women, who are the majority in the national population, made up only 13% of the delegate strength. As the McGovern Report concluded, "The delegates to the 1968 Democratic National Convention, in short, were predominately white, male, middleaged, and at least middle class".

In an attempt to remedy this situation, several reforms were advanced. Among these were: a limitation on mandatory "participation fees" (which sometimes totaled as high as $500 per delegate in one delegation); a rule forbidding racial discrimination in delegate selection; and adoption of a general policy encouraging representation in the convention of minority groups, young people and women in rough proportion to their representation in the population. Certain reforms were also designed to prevent selection of delegates in a "smoke-filled room," for example, by a rule requiring timely and adequate notice of all local meetings at which delegates were to be selected, and a rule that no more than 10% of a state's delegation could be handpicked by the local state committee.

Critics desiring more drastic change have argued that this last recommendation does not go far enough, and that the Baker v. Carr one-person, one-vote standard should be applied to the convention delegate selection process. (See Chapter V for discussion of this principle.) While several court cases have been brought protesting delegate selection procedures, the courts, thus far, appear reluctant to decide what they consider to be a strictly "political question."

While the recommendations of the McGovern Commission have not always been heeded, the report has outlined reforms which could go a long way towards implementing democratic principles in the selection of candidates as well as in voter participation. (The first reports on delegates chosen for the 1972 Democratic convention reveal that people previously uninvolved in political affairs were selected, including more women, young people and minority group members -- even though their numbers are still short of their total of the national population.) No comparable recommendations have yet emerged from the Republican Party, but the Democratic Party's attention to these serious inequities appears to have had a sobering effect on delegate selection in both parties all over the country.

Chapter 4

CAN YOU VOTE WHEN ABSENT FROM HOME?

Sociologists, census analysts and other students of the urban and rural scene may differ sharply about the causes for transfigurations in American society during the 20th Century, but there is complete accord on one central fact--the constant movement of Americans from one place to another. As new and easier means of transportation grew, as vacation and education periods lengthened, as the expanding (and shrinking) economy forced job relocation, and as the tight reins of home and parental influence loosened, more and more Americans were *on the road". This phenomenon of American life, which shows no signs of lessening, literally places millions of voters away from their home communities on Election Day.

The democratic imperative of voting participation made it essential that some machinery be provided for them in absentia to join in the election process. The mechanism devised was the absentee ballot, which over the years has been widely used. The rise of absentee voters has definitely affected the outcome of elections in particular states. In the hotly contested 1960 Kennedy-Nixon battle, California's 40 electoral votes were initially in the Kennedy column by a 20,000 vote margin. When the 243,000 absentee ballots were counted, Nixon had carried the state by 35,000 votes.

The Absentee Civilian Voter

Since Vermont, as far back as 1896, won the honor of being the first state to adopt a civilian absentee voting law providing that a qualified voter could, upon presentation of a certificate, vote at any polling place within the state, all states have experimented with absentee voting systems. These voting arrange-

_____

*In the opinion of Richard Scammon, the experienced political analyst, the civilian and military absentee vote is definitely increasing. In a discussion with the authors, he said: *I would think there has been a marked rise in such votes over the last 25 years, due to population mobility and the growth of literate voters."

ments enable citizens, if they plan to be absent from the county or state on Election Day, to cast their ballots before the election, either in person or by mail.

At one time absentee voting was limited only to certain elections. Today all states provide for some form of absentee voting in primary or general elections, a logical development showing the importance of the franchise in broadening and deepening this cardinal facet of the democratic system. Only Connecticut, Delaware, New York, North Carolina, and Rhode Island restrict absentee voting to general elections. South Carolina leaves the question of primary absentee voting in the hands of the political party or subdivision conducting the election, but points the way toward absentee participation by this statutory language affecting primary and special elections:

Boards of Registration and all other election officials of this state shall cooperate with such authorities to the end that the right to vote may be preserved for all persons [permitted to vote absentee].

There are obvious and serious difficulties connected with an absentee voting system. The danger of fraud, a possibility in any election, increases when ballots are marked outside the carefully regularized procedure of the polling place. The alternative arrangements required also mean greater expense and more work for the election officials. They must provide special absentee ballots, make them available well in advance of the election, arrange for their official distribution, establish a receiving agent for the marked ballots, distribute them to the proper polling place, verify their validity, and assure that they are properly tabulated in the final count.

Another, albeit minor problem compared to the administrative headaches, is the quandary of challenging an absentee voter. Usually challenges are made prior to Election Day as absentee lists are posted before the election. But refuting the challenge or providing for appeal when the challenge is sustained is difficult when the voter is not present at the polls. These drawbacks are clearly outweighed, however, by the thrust of constitutional guarantees, that as many citizens as possible should vote in elections, the keystone to democracy's survival and growth.

Eligibility Rules

All states forestall the possibility that voters will cast an absentee ballot simply for their own convenience by describing in detail the electors who are eligible to vote by absentee ballot. The liberality of most of these provisions attests to the states acceptance of the proposition advanced by students of the voting process who maintain that eligibility requirements should never be so complicated or overly restrictive as to preclude voting by a large number of people who rightfully deserve the privilege. Most states agree that there is obviously little virtue in providing absentee voting opportunities at all if excessively rigid or technical provisions discourage the majority of voters from even attempting to comply.

The election codes of all but three states (Alabama, Mississipi and South Carolina) have very broad eligibility provisions which, although phrased differently in different laws, essentially afford absentee voting privileges to anyone who is absent for any reason from the election district or state on Election Day. Such flexibility matches the views of most voting experts who maintain that the reason for a voter's absence is immaterial since the purpose of the absentee vote is simply to meet the needs of the voter, not to favor one group of electors over another.

What limitations are imposed fall on certain specified groups which cannot get to the polls because their occupation or special condition keeps them away from home. Alabama, for example, confines absentee voting to military personnel, disabled veterans, members of the Merchant Marine and others who are absent because of their business or occupation. Mississippi permits only the military, disabled war veterans and persons employed in the transportation industry to vote in absentia. South Carolina limits absentee balloting to members of the armed forces and Merchant Marine, students, Red Cross and USO workers attached to the military, members or employees of any U.S. government department working overseas, and those employed in transportation industries.

Other special situations are recognized by the states. With the exception of Mississippi and South Carolina, all states allow for absentee voting by voters who are unable to appear at the polls in person because they are ill, infirm, or physically disabled. Usually such an elector must submit a physician's certificate or a statement by a practitioner of Christian Science which attests to the legitimacy of the claimed physical disability or sickness. Certain states (Arizona, California, Colorado, Connecticut, Florida, Hawaii, Illinois, Maine, Michigan, Minnesota, New Jersey, Tennessee, Texas, Vermont and Wisconsin) also expressly grant absent voting rights to electors who cannot personally go to the polls on Election Day because of religious tenets or observance of religious holidays. Typically, students are also a favored group. In all states but Mississippi, students living outside their usual place of residence are permitted access to absentee ballots.

Not all absentee voters have an easy time in exercising the franchise. United States citizens and their spouses and dependents, who temporarily reside outside the territorial limits of the United States and the District of Columbia, face special problems because many states do not extend to them either absentee voting or absentee registration rights. Congress took account of this problem in 1968 when it passed Public Law 90-343, amending the Federal Voting Assistance Act of 1955 (discussed below under The Absentee Military Voter), to include in its recommendations to the states that any citizens temporarily residing overseas be included among those eligible to register and vote absentee. Since then, 14 states (Arkansas, California, Georgia, Hawaii, Kansas, Massachusetts, Minnesota, Montana, New York, Nebraska, New Mexico, Oregon, Texas and Washington) have complied with the request by expressly including such citizens in their non-civilian absentee voter laws, thus effectively permitting absentee registration and voting via the military's Federal Post Card Application. Other states which allow absentee registration and absentee voting by any absent elector also effectively sanction the voting of overseas citizens, but make no special arrangements such as the FPCA for such electors. This situation calls for legislative reform in furtherance of the principle of an expanding electorate. Laws should be passed to convenience any elector residing overseas by including him or her in a state's non-civilian absentee voter category.

Since all the intricacies of election codes are not known to the average citizen, it is a good idea when there is doubt about voting eligibility to consult the Secretary of State in your state of residence or the local election official for advice. The reader is also referred to the state-by-state description of absentee and voting provisions in Appendix III.

Procedural Details

All states follow essentially the same general procedure for obtaining and marking an absentee ballot, but such specific details as time of application, the election officers to whom the

69

voter applies and the date for return of the ballot are peculiar to each state.

Shielding the election system against voting tricks is of central importance, so safeguards against dishonest voting must be incorporated into any absentee voting plan. The keys to such protection are carefully drawn provisions that allow only qualified voters to obtain absentee ballots and mark them accurately, honestly and without collusion. To meet the first requirement, all absentee voting systems require the elector, or in some states, his or her representative (a friend or relative) to apply directly to an election official to obtain the ballot. The official checks the voter's record in the official files and furnishes a ballot only if the elector is found to be validly registered.

Thirty-two states (Alabama, Arkansas, California - in some counties, Connecticut, Delaware, Florida, Illinois, Indiana, Iowa, Kansas, Kentucky, Maryland, Michigan, Minnesota, Missouri, Montana, Nebraska, New Mexico, New York, North Carolina, North Dakota, Ohio, Pennsylvania, Rhode Island, South Carolina, South Dakota, Tennessee, Texas, Utah, Vermont, Virginia, West Virginia) re-inforce the precaution by making official application forms available to the voter at the local election board. Indeed some states will only accept absentee voter applications made on these forms. Other states are not that picky, and will take the application if it contains the necessary information. Usually a simple letter, postcard or even a telephone call is sufficient. To be sure, absentee voters in states having an official application form should consult their local election officials to determine the correct procedure.

In most instances, the absentee ballot application contains an affidavit form which must be completed and sworn to by the applicant in the presence of a notary public or other officer legally authorized to administer oaths. The affidavit declares that the information on the application concerning the voter's permanent voting residence, qualifications to vote by absentee ballot and biographical data are accurate.

Once the application and, where required, its notarized affidavit, are received by the appropriate election officer, the voter's name is checked against the permanent registration records. If the registration is in good standing, and the applicant's signature compares accurately with the signature in the registration files, the election officer at the appropriate time before the election (and the time varies considerably from state to state) sends the voter all of the necessary ballots along with instructions for marking and returning them. The voter receives the ballots enclosed in an official envelope, sometimes called a voucher envelope. The voucher is enclosed in an outside or carrier wrapper in which the ballot and its envelope are to be returned.

The ballot materials usually include an instruction to take the ballot and an accompanying affidavit stating that the named elector actually voted to a notary public or other officer authorized to administer oaths. In the presence of that officer, the voter marks the ballot without, however, divulging to the officer for which candidate the vote was cast. The ballot is then deposited in the official carrier envelope and sealed. In some states, the notary public is required to place the official seal on the voucher envelope, in others on the carrier envelope. The envelope is then mailed, preferably by registered or certified mail, to the appropriate election official; in some states it may be delivered in person or by the voter's representative if this proves more convenient for the voter.

The absentee voter should mail the ballot as early as possible, for many states require that it must arrive at the office of the registrar or election board in time to be delivered to the appropriate polling place before the polls close on Election Day. Since four states (North Carolina, Oklahoma, Ohio and Pennsylvania) require that absentee ballots be in the hands of the election officers several days before the election, voters in these states should carefully check the regulations. If an absentee ballot arrives after the prescribed deadline, it is marked invalid and placed in a special box or file without being opened. All such ballots are kept for several months after an election in case any investigation of the validity of the vote is undertaken.

All the care and caution taken to preserve the integrity of the absentee vote would be meaningless if these ballots were not honestly counted. Various techniques are employed to ensure the probity of the balloting. In most states, absentee ballots are specially numbered with the voucher and carrier envelopes often correspondingly marked. This makes it possible to check not only the authenticity of the ballot which is marked but also which of the absentee ballots are returned.

In some states, of which Nevada is an example, if a voter applies for an absentee ballot but does not return it (that is, does not vote), the registration is cancelled, and the individual must re-register in order to recover standing as a qualified elector. In states which purge registration lists of electors who do not vote for a period of years, it is necessary to keep track of which absentee voter does, in fact, cast a ballot and thus meets the qualification for consistent voting. The most conclusive check on the honesty of the ballot is, of course, the affidavit to which the voter swears when filling out the ballot, for a voter is liable to conviction for perjury if false information is given on this voucher.

An absentee ballot may be challenged either before the election or at the polls on various grounds: establishing the falsity of information about voting qualifications; proving that the voter was not, in fact, absent from the voting district on Election Day or did not fulfill other necessary requirements; or showing that the absentee is not a registered voter in good standing. In case of challenge, the absentee ballot is put aside and the voter is notified that the vote has been contested. If possible, a personal appearance can be made to defend the right of franchise or necessary information may be sent. Generally the challenged absentee ballot cannot be verified by the voter on Election Day, but this is not important unless the final count is so close as to be significantly changed by the absentee count.

What happens if the elector casts an absentee ballot and then returns home on Election Day --making him or her able to cast a ballot in person? In a number of states voting at the polls is permitted, provided the election officials have not completed their totalling of the absentee vote. If a voter dies after the absentee ballot has been cast, that ballot is not counted if the election officials receive information of the death in time to discount the vote.

Pre-election Voting

A number of states, including Alabama, Louisiana, North Dakota and Texas, accommodate civilian voters who anticipate their absence on Election Day. They arrange for the voter to cast a ballot at the office of the local election clerk before the regular election date. In states where this is possible, the voter may usually apply in person at the election office as soon as the ballots are printed (usually several weeks before the election), receive a ballot and vote it on the spot in the presence of the election officer. Such ballots

72

are held until Election Day when they are distributed to the appropriate polling place to be counted with the regularly marked ballots.

Certain time periods are fixed for pre-election voting. Louisiana permits an absentee voter to mark the ballot 30 days prior to election at the office of the Clerk of the District Court of the parish or at the office of the Civil Sheriff in the Parish of Orleans. In Alabama, businessmen expecting to be absent on Election Day may apply to the board of registrars not less than 30 days before the election to have their names placed on a list of absentee voters. Such electors may vote in person at the county registrar's office between the 20th and 5th day before the election. North Dakota permits pre-election voting by anyone anticipating absence who is present in the county after the official ballots have been printed. To vote in person before the election, the elector has to apply to the county auditor for instructions. Texas allows a voter, at the discretion of the election clerk, to vote an absentee ballot in person between 2 P.M. and 8 P.M. on the last Saturday and Sunday, or other Saturday and Sunday, of the absentee voting period.

Absentee Voting in Primaries

Every state now provides for a primary election for at least a limited class of statewide officers. General qualifications for voters in such elections are discussed in Chapter 3 ("How Does the Voting System Work?"). In those states which sanction civilian absentee voting in primary elections (all but Connecticut, Delaware, New York, North Carolina, Rhode Island, and South Carolina), the procedures followed are the same as in the general election. Ostensibly, the reason for these six states barring civilians from casting absentee votes in primaries is the conviction that primary elections need the involved personal participation of the electorate. This rests on the assumption that the bitter battles waged in primaries over local issues somehow requires an elector to be on the scene to weigh the relative merits of candidates' arguments.

But, much more likely, the prohibition is based on a hard financial fact, the administrative expense of processing what would prove to be only a relatively small number of votes. While such a disqualification may seem reasonable, election and constitutional experts offer the counter argument that failure to provide for absentee voting in any election--general or pri-

73

mary--may well violate the Constitution's equal protection clause by unreasonably disfranchising an absent voter.

The Absentee Military Voter

With millions of American men and women serving in the Armed Forces, it is abundantly clear that a system for enfranchising such persons absent from their homes on Election Day because of military duty is a palpable need. But even before the United States assumed far-flung military commitments over the last several decades, federal and state governments had adopted measures to facilitate the casting of ballots by service personnel.

As early as the Civil War, 11 northern states allowed soldiers who were residents of those states to vote in the field or by proxy. Actually, a fairly large number of soldiers received furloughs in the election of 1864 so that they could return home to vote. Popular pressure for national absentee voting laws arose during the Spanish American War and then in the First World War as the size of military forces serving overseas increased. But, although absentee voting bills were introduced, in neither conflict did Congress enact such legislation.

By the beginning of World War II, however, a number of states had passed laws enabling members of the military to vote by absentee ballot. And in 1942 Congress, motivated by an interest primarily to extend suffrage to service people from states without absentee voting regulations, approved the Servicemen's Voting Act. This law accorded soldiers the right to vote in absentia in Presidential and Congressional elections and exempted them from state requirements governing personal registration or the payment of poll taxes in these elections. Congress amended the earlier legislation in 1944 by strongly urging more state help to military absentees and providing a federal war ballot for military voters to cast in Presidential and Congressional elections.

Despite the federal ballot, military participation in voting was only half that of the civilian population of voting age. According to a report of the American Political Science Association, only 2,691,160 of the 9,255,000 eligible military voters actually voted in 1944. This amounted to 30% of the total number of service personnel, in comparison to the 60% of eligible civilians who went to the polls. The military vote totalled only five and one-half percent of the total popular vote in that Presidential election. The voting performance in the last four Presidential elections has been better (32.5%, 1956; 39.4%, 1960; 51.3%, 1964; and 46.2%, 1968), but the general voting record is not satisfactory.

During World War II the various state laws operated with widely varying degrees of success. With the end of World War II, some peacetime guarantee of absentee voting rights for persons still serving in the armed forces was obviously necessary and the spotlight focussed on Congress. However, some legislators and state officials expressed persistent concern that broadened federal legislation might threaten the power of the states to conduct their own elections, so in 1946 Congress passed legislation which essentially returned control over absentee voting to the states. The 1946 law did, however, move the federal government significantly into the picture by creating a federal postcard application for an absentee ballot that could be filed with state authorities, and authorizing special arrangements to facilitate the procurement and return of ballots by service personnel in remote areas. The federal law also continued the exemptions from requirements for personal registration and payment of poll taxes which might be imposed on civilians in their resident states.

A decade later, as the intensified conflict between the Soviet Union and the United States inevitably led to the establishment of major American military installations all over the world, Congress took additional steps to help the military absentee voter. It adopted the Federal Voting Assistance Act of 1955 which proposed various suggestions to the states for boosting voting and also authorized the President to aid certain classes of voters whose duty or service required their absence on Election Day. This was done by creating a special Federal Voting Assistance Program coordinated by the Secretary of Defense. Individuals entitled to special federal assistance were

(1) Members of the Armed Forces while in the active service, and their spouses and dependents.

(2) Members of the Merchant Marine of the United States, and their spouses and dependents.

(3) Civilian employees of the United States in all categories serving outside the territorial limits of the several States of the United States, and the District of Columbia, and their spouses and dependents when residing with or accompanying them . . .

(4) Members of religious groups or welfare agencies assisting members of the Armed Forces, who are officially attached to and serving with the Armed Forces, and their spouses and dependents.

Most importantly, the 1955 Act also strengthened the Federal Post Card Application (FPCA) idea initiated in the 1946 law. While the earlier statute allowed such an application for an absentee ballot, the 1955 law suggested that the states accept the FPCA for purposes of both registration and an absentee ballot request by armed forces personnel and members of the above-named related groups. State legislative reform followed and currently all states accept the FPCA as a proper application for an absentee ballot. Moreover, 13 states (Colorado, Hawaii, Indiana, Massachusetts, Minnesota, Montana, New Hampshire, New Mexico, New York, North Carolina, South Dakota, Tennessee, Texas) additionally validate the FPCA for registration purposes as well. The FPCA contains virtually all the information a voting registrar would need in order to issue an absentee ballot. It designates fully the place and type of election for which an absentee ballot is being requested; contains all relevant information regarding the applicant's name, permanent and military addresses, and voting qualifications; and lastly provides for notorization of the application by an individual authorized to administer oaths. In most states, this group includes any commissioned officer or non-commissioned officer of the rank of sergeant or petty officer.

The door opened to increased military voting by extending absentee voting rights to the four groups named in the Federal Voting Assistance Act of 1955 has been accepted in 30 states either by specific reference or by granting any overseas elector the right to vote by the FPCA. (Arkansas, Colorado, Florida, Georgia, Hawaii, Idaho, Illinois, Iowa, Kansas, Kentucky, Louisiana, Maine, Maryland, Massachusetts, Minnesota, Missouri, Montana, Nebraska, Nevada, New Hampshire, New Mexico, North Dakota, Pennsylvania, Tennessee, Texas, Utah, Vermont, Washinton, Wisconsin and Wyoming). Certain qualifications exist in other states, however. Ten states (Alaska, California, Connecticut, Delaware, Mississippi, Oklahoma, Rhode Island, South Dakota, Texas and West Virginia) permit voting by only three of the four groups, excluding either civilian government employees serving overseas, or members of the Merchant Marine or religious or welfare agencies attached to the armed forces. While all states grant FPCA absentee voting privileges to members of the armed forces, Arizona and Oregon do not expressly extend this privilege to military spouses and dependents. Three states, Arizona, Indiana and North Carolina, grant absentee military voting rights only to military personnel and members of the Merchant Marine. Most states exclude Merchant Marine members who serve on vessels on inland waterways or the Great Lakes.

Only four states, Alabama, New York, Ohio and Virginia, limit the definition of those eligible to cast a military ballot to electors in actual military service (and their spouses and dependents). In these states, however, the civilian absentee voting provisions seem broad enough to include the families of service personnel and other electors who may be working with the armed forces in a civilian capacity. The chart on page 107 presents a complete state-by-state breakdown of military-connected groups affected by absentee voting provisions.

The liberalized attitude shown toward accepting absentee military personnel as regular voters is reflected in the states' absentee registration procedures. Twenty-three states either permit voting by military and related groups without prior registration, or accept a completed FPCA as evidence of complying with absentee registration requirements. In 14 states (Arizona, California, Connecticut, Delaware, Florida, Georgia, Kentucky, Michigan, Mississippi, Nebraska, Pennsylvania, South Carolina, Virginia and West Virginia) receipt of an FPCA application will bring the elector an official absentee registration form from the local registrar which must be filled out and returned. In 8 states, a military voter is automatically registered when officials accept the executed affidavit on the ballot-return envelope. In Alabama, Alaska, Louisiana, Maine and Nevada, military voters request the official state registration form prior to applying for an absentee ballot via the FPCA. The lack of a uniform state registration procedure, such as use of the FPCA, has been noted by critics of the Federal Voting Assistance Act who charge that the wide variations create great confusion which limits opportunities for voting.

There are administrative headaches in handling absentee voting applications covering vast distances, as illustrated by the state laws governing time limits in which applications can be submitted. While 16 states permit military absentee ballot requests at any time, 13 states allow applications as early as 90 days before election, 8 states will entertain requests as early as 60 days before, and 8 states set at least a 30-day time period.

But the real test of military absentee voting laws rests not simply on statutory language, but on how the laws are actually implemented and whether they actually succeed in bringing the ballot to military voters. The high echelons of the Department of Defense seem committed to making the Federal Voting Assistance Act work. A 1971 directive of the Department speaks of encouraging "voters to avail themselves of the absentee voting privileges provided by the several states." (Department of Defense Directive 1000.4, July 10, 1971.) This is amplified by specifying in detail the procedures and conditions under which service personnel may obtain and complete voting forms and other material.

Voting is stimulated by getting and disseminating current absentee voting information from each state; holding ceremonies on Armed Forces Voters Day in late September of each election year to emphasize the responsibility of voting; and reporting to the President and Congress on the success of the absentee voting program. Individual assistance to voters is given by advising on how to determine legal residence and voting age requirements and expediting the transmission, handling and delivery of absentee voting mail (including delivery of absentee voting material by priority air mail).

As intimidation of military voters is an inherent danger in the military system of tight control and discipline, great emphasis is placed in the directives on safeguarding "the integrity and secrecy of the ballot." In directing that "all necessary steps shall be taken to prevent fraud and to protect voters against coercion of any sort," the Department of Defense bars influencing

> any member of the Armed Forces to vote or not to vote for any particular candidate, or to . . . march to any . . . place of voting.

Members of the armed forces cannot be polled either before or after the election about their choice of candidates. The warning against influencing the military voter does not cover "free discussion regarding political issues or candidates for the public office."

Despite the good intentions and high-sounding phrases, the voting statistics demonstrate that the military voting record is a very poor one.

According to a sample survey conducted by the Youth Citizenship Fund, Inc., a non-profit educational group, only 26.5% of those in uniform voted in the 1970 elections. Granted that voting interest dwindles in non-presidential election years, the survey covering 35 Army, Navy, Air Force, Marine and Coast Guard bases reveals that the enlightened written policies and directives promulgated by the Pentagon rarely receive top drawer attention by lower echelon military commanders in the field.

The figures for the last four general bi-ennial elections show some rise (18.7%, 1958; 20.1%, 1962; 27.4%, 1966, and 26.5% in 1970) but the record still falls far short of what might be achieved if the energy and interest of the field commanders could be harnessed to promote more vigorously the absentee vote drive. The fault lies not only in the attitude of these commanders, for the 1955 voting assistance law specifically grants military field leaders broad latitude in determining what priority the voting program receives. As the Youth Citizenship Fund, Inc. said in a report on the 1955 Act:

> There is little to encourage a military commander to take care that even the limited voting program outlined in the Act is conducted properly when the enacting legislation permits a Commander to make a "good faith" decision that his post or unit has no time for a voting program.

The dismal voting performance may reflect not only a failure to follow up at the lower levels, but the general malaise and disaffection from democratic processes that many observers of the military scene report. In a commendable effort to remedy the situation, the Youth Citizenship Fund, Inc. is now developing special joint campaigns with the military voting Task Force aimed at intensifying interest in observing both the letter and the spirit of the 1955 voting assistance law.

Chapter 5

HOW PURE IS THE ELECTION PROCESS?

In highlighting the cardinal role of the franchise in having citizens actively participate in and control the affairs of their government, the previous chapters of this book have featured two central themes: (1) the profound voting changes adopted as part of the country's social revolution in the last two decades; and (2) the technical, procedural aspects of voting.

This information presents a voting canvass which paints in the rights and responsibilities of electors within a democratic system. But the picture is incomplete unless major trends and developments are sketched which show the imperfections in the election process and the efforts being made to rectify them -- to fulfill the democratic potential and ideal of that process. The goal is to improve the electoral structure so that the political system can function with greater equality and fairness for all.

Apportionment

Behind the oft-quoted phrase of the Declaration of Independence,

All Men are created equal, that they are endowed by their Creator with certain inalienable Rights, that among these are Life, Liberty and the Pursuit of Happiness.

lies the essence of American democracy. The central thrust of this philosophical assertion is equality, that no human being is more valuable than another, that each man or woman, regardless of wealth, social status, physical ability, or other characteristic, has the same right to life and freedom. And our law must protect this right.

This basic concept is manifested in the Constitution's provision that the House of Representatives is to be elected "by the People" -- clearly implying that each person is to receive one, and only one, vote. Under our democratic framework, when the ballots are collected and counted, the poorest tenant farmer should have the same voice as the richest urban millionaire. The fact that one voter, because of wealth or other advantage, might possess more political power or influence than another voter is irrelevant in deciding that each has the same weight when he or she pulls the voting lever.

The political realities of American history show that this precept was not always honored. In the eighteen hundreds, less than 10% of the American population were qualified to vote. "Sex, color, property holdings, payment of taxes, past servitude, and conviction of 'infamous crimes' were all considered legitimate limitations on the 'privilege' of suffrage."* Until very recently, persons could be lawfully disfranchised upon failure to pass a state-imposed literacy test. Black men and women and other racial minorities could be refused the ballot by dubious administrative practices or, more often, by harrassment and outright intimidation. Yet, despite these and other anomalies, the fundamental idea remains that each qualified elector possesses the same voice, the same power, as any other qualified elector when he or she enters the voting booth.

The guarantee of an equal vote, however, covers several elements, including fair apportionment. As Supreme Court Justice William O. Douglas stated in South v. Peters (1950):

There is more to the right to vote than the right to mark a piece of paper and drop it in a box or the right to pull a lever in a voting booth. The right to vote includes the right to have the ballot counted . . . It also includes the right to have the vote counted at full value without dilution or discount.

The idea of apportionment is relatively simple. Visualize two congressional districts, each having one representative in the Congress. Voter A votes in the first district where there is a population of 5,000 people. Voter B votes in the second district where there is a population of 10,000 people. But A's vote counts twice as much as B's because the Congressman in the first district represents only 5,000 people, while the Congressman in the second district represents 10,000 people. The diagram below illustrates the problem.

*DuFresne, "The Case for Allowing Convicted Mafiosi to Vote for Judges": Beyond Green v. Board of Election of New York City, 19 DE PAUL L REV 112, 113 (1969) quoting Story, Our Unalienable Rights, p. 47 (1965).

Voter B's vote has been diluted, not because he or she voted more times than A (both only voted once), but because A lives in a less populated district than B and thus has a larger voice in electing the representative. The advantage to A is obvious. Because the district is smaller, each individual residing there will receive more than his or her per capita share of governmental programs, services or funds. More importantly, voter A will wield twice the political influence as Voter B, permitting the former's point of view and political preferences to be more affirmatively presented.

The question of malapportionment is not a new factor in the political scene. It has been a feature of our system throughout our history. What is new is the awakening consciousness to the scope of the problem, and how existing apportionment arrangements solidified the control of political forces in the more rural regions. This awareness was generated by the gradual urbanization of America which has shifted masses of people from rural sections to the cities. The chart, (p. 110) taken from Bureau of Census figures, tabulates this population shift from 1 out of 4 Americans living in urban areas in 1870 to 3 out of 4 living there a century later.

Theoretically, the country was not bereft of a mechanism for producing fair apportionment. The founding fathers wisely incorporated in Article I of the Constitution the requirement of a decennial census, one of whose purposes is to reapportion federal congressional districts. State legislatures also have the power to reapportion the districts from which state senators and representatives are elected. A large number of these bodies, however, tightly controlled by rural interests reluctant to relinquish their power, turned a deaf ear to repeated calls for reshaping legislative districts. Given the rewards of political puissance, rural legislators understandably were not eager to carve out new urban districts that in some cases meant abolishing their own.

Years of persistent political debate produced no change, and as legislatures remained adamantly opposed to urban-sponsored measures to alleviate the mounting volume of city problems, recourse was sought in the courts. At first the Supreme Court was unwilling to decide what it regarded as a "political question", and turned back constant challenges to malapportioned legislatures. But the pendulum finally swung in 1961 when the Supreme Court agreed to hear the case of a group of Tennessee citizens who claimed that they were being denied equal protection of the laws because their votes were being diluted by a 1901 Tennessee statute which "capriciously" apportioned the seats in the Tennessee General Assembly among the state's 95 counties--none of which had been subsequently reapportioned.

Lawyers representing the state of Tennessee not only argued that the Supreme Court lacked the power to decide a political question, but also that the Constitution did not require adherence to the one-person, one-vote principle. There are many indices of political power, they contended, and the Constitution itself sanctions malapportionment by creating a Senate composed of two Senators from each state, regardless of population.

These arguments, however, proved futile. In 1962, the Supreme Court handed down its landmark Baker v. Carr decision, undoubtedly one of the most famous and far-reaching cases in American constitutional law. The high court held that the Tennessee citizens were entitled to judicial relief if their claims were found to be true. The effect of this ruling was to put all states on notice that failure to reapportion legislative districts was now a violation of the Constitution, and that the federal courts stood ready to vindicate the rights of citizens whose votes were being diluted by malapportionment.

Supreme Court decisions followed that more precisely defined the constitutional requirements of apportionment. In Reynolds v. Sims, the Court decided that one-person, one-vote required both houses of a bicameral state legislature to be apportioned. The Court noted that the Constitution's creation of a malapportioned U.S. Senate was the result of a unique political compromise and could not be the measuring rod for determining the requisites of equal protection. Chief Justice Earl Warren, after reviewing the history of the Court's protection of voting rights, emphasized the inter-connection between those rights and apportionment:

> [H]istory has seen a continuing expansion of the scope of the right of suffrage in this country. The right to vote freely for the candidate of one's choice is the essence of a democratic society, and any restrictions on that right strike at the heart of a representative government. And the right of suffrage can be denied by a debasement or dilution of the weight of a citizen's vote just as effectively as by wholly prohibiting the free exercise of the franchise.

The heart of the reapportionment decisions is substantial adherence to the one-person, one-vote formula, not mathematical precision. This applies not only to houses of a state legislature but to any elected body performing "legislative functions". While the Supreme Court has not clearly defined what is meant by a "legislative function", it seems fairly clear that any body with extensive law-making powers, such as the power to levy taxes, is governed by the one-person, one-vote requirement. The high court's rulings were not absolute. They did not stifle "experimentation" by political units (such as school boards) which perform only "administrative" functions.

While Baker v. Carr and its companion decisions became the law of the land, the apportionment controversy was far from ended. For obvious political reasons, the executive branch of the federal government refrained from enforcing the Supreme Court's mandate and left the states to fashion their own solutions. The result has been a continuing swirl of political conflict over the adequacy of particular reapportionment plans and a steady flow of litigation to compel adherence to the one-person one-vote principle.

But the political and legal wrangling has not undercut the clear meaning of the Supreme Court's precedent-making decisions. Following the court's direction, since Baker v. Carr all 50 states have reapportioned their state and congressional districts to equalize the urban-rural population composition. In fact, since the 1970 census figures were reported, all states have again rearranged their congressional districts and all but five their state districts in order to achieve a better equality of franchise.

Electoral College Reform

The inherent inequities in malapportionment are aligned with a unique voting peculiarity contained in the Constitution itself. When the Constitution was drafted at the 1787 Constitutional Convention, there was fear of entrusting to the masses of people direct power to elect the executive head of the government. After heated debate over the issue of complete or partial democracy, a compromise measure was adopted which granted the people a limited voice--but not final authority--over selection of the President.

A select group, the Electoral College, was created in which each state is represented by as many Presidential electors as it has Senators and Representatives in the Congress. A majority vote of the Electoral College is required to elect the President. If no candidate receives a majority, the election is thrown into the House of Representatives which has the sole power to select the chief executive, with each state having one and only one vote.

As the nation grew, and as the notion of increased citizen participation in voting took hold in the 20th Century, the Electoral College has been severely criticized on a number of grounds.

The major complaints fall into these six categories:

(1) Under the law or the custom of every state, the Presidential candidate who wins a plurality of votes in the state re-

ceives all of that state's electoral votes. Thus, whether a candidate receives 51% or 99% of the popular vote within a state, the candidate ends up with the same number of electoral votes. In 1968, President Nixon captured all of California's 40 electoral votes despite the fact that Senator Humphrey won 44.7% of the popular vote. Conversely, Senator Humphrey swept 100% of New York's 43 electoral votes with only 49.8% of that state's voters behind him. This "general ticket" system (sometimes called the "unit rule" method) of counting electoral votes allows a handful of large states to wield enormous political influence over the candidates and platforms of the major parties. New York and California, which now possess 41 and 45 electoral votes, respectively, for example, often have had a disproportionately large say in the composition of the national ticket. The danger of large-state domination was aptly pictured in author Theodore White's (The Making of the President, 1960, page 246) description of John Kennedy's 1960 election strategy:

Nine large states hold 237 of the 269 electoral votes necessary to elect a President. If those could be swept, and if another 60 or 70 could be added by Lyndon Johnson in the Old South, and if a few more solid New England or Midwestern States could be counted in--then the election would be won handily.

The "general ticket" system also has been scored for discouraging minority groups from voting because of the winner-take-all nature of the contest. This contention may no longer hold true, however, now that minorities are marshaling their political strength. In many states, their vote can tip the balance for or against a candidate.

(2) Because of the all-or-nothing feature, even though a Presidential candidate wins a popular vote majority it is possible for the candidate to lose the election. This has actually happened three times in our history, in the Presidential elections of 1824, 1876, and 1888. (In 1824, the winner, John Quincy Adams, received 105,321 votes. Andrew Jackson, one of the losers, polled 155,872 votes. No one received a majority of electoral votes and the House of Representatives chose Adams. In the election of 1876 challenger Samuel Tilden received 4,284,757 votes. The winner, Rutherford B. Hayes, received 4,033,950 votes. The 1888 election saw Benjamin Harrison defeat Grover Cleveland even though the popular vote favored Cleveland by 5,540,050 to 5,444,337.) In fifteen elections, a shift of less than 1% of the

national votes cast would have made candidates with a minority of the popular votes President. Illustrating how the Electoral College system undermines the basic principle of democratic government, consent of the governed, in this century three Presidents have been elected by a majority of electoral votes, but only by a minority of the voters: Woodrow Wilson in 1912; Harry S. Truman in 1948; and Richard M. Nixon in 1968. The tables (p. 111), computed from the results of the 1960 and 1968 Presidential elections, exemplify the problem. In 1968 Richard M. Nixon received 43.4% of the popular vote, but a whopping 55.9% of the Electoral College votes. In 1960, John F. Kennedy won handily with 56.4% of the electoral vote, even though he received the approval of only 49.7% of the people.

(3)   Because each state receives a minimum of three electoral votes, based on two Senators and at least one Representative, the one-person, one-vote principle often is seriously infringed. For example, under the 1970 census figures, Alaska with a population of 304,067 has three electoral votes, or one for each 101,356 persons; California, with a 1970 population of 20,098,863 has 45 electoral votes, or one for every 446,641 persons.

(4)   The problem of the "faithless elector" exists, despite the fact that the laws of many states purport to require Presidential electors to cast their ballots for the state's popular vote winner. This is not simply a theoretical danger. In 1968, a Republican elector from North Carolina pledged to the Nixon-Agnew ticket, actually cast his vote in the Electoral College for the Wallace-LeMay slate.

(5)   The "runoff" procedure in the House of Representatives is highly inadequate, under the one-person, one-vote criterion. Allowing the House, when no candidate receives a majority of the Electoral College, to elect the President by having each state cast one vote obviously runs afoul of the no-dilution-of-the-vote principle. Moreover, this procedure would undoubtedly permit those few states whose voters backed a third, minority party candidate to exert tremendous political leverage. Their "swing votes" in the House contest would be wholly out of proportion to their populations. This is exactly what the country would have faced if in 1968 President Nixon had lost the states of Illinois and Missouri by a mere shift of 72,000 votes (less than one-thousandth of one per cent of the total vote cast in the election).

(6)   The Electoral College system makes no provision in the event of a candidate's untimely death. A candidate may die

before Election Day, as did James Sherman, the 1912 Vice-Presidential candidate; after Election Day but before the December meeting of the Electoral College, as did Horace Greeley, the 1872 Presidential candidate; or after the casting of the electoral votes but before their counting when Congress convenes. If any of these contingencies occur, serious questions arise as to whether votes can be counted for a dead candidate. The present system is silent in regard to these possibilities.

Electoral College reform has been a favorite topic of debate for political scientists over the years. But the argument waxed even hotter after the 1968 Presidential election when President Nixon's small popular plurality and George Wallace's third-party candidacy brought the theoretical inadequacies of the Electoral College perilously close to actual reality. In response to the cry for change, several constitutional amendments were proposed centering on the idea of direct election of the President.

One advocated by the American Bar Association's Commission on Electoral Reform actually passed the House of Representatives in 1969 (by a 339 to 70 vote) but failed in the Senate. Providing for popular election of the President and Vice-President, this proposal included a run-off election between the two top candidates if no candidate received at least 40% of the votes cast. Although eliminating the Electoral College and the potential power of the House of Representatives in a runoff contest, the popular runoff election, in effect, sanctioned the election of a minority President. The eventual winner could actually be the choice of only a small fraction of the electorate, because splinter groups and small political parties, while each receiving only a fraction of the vote, would be encouraged to all work together towards being included as one of the "top two" candidates.

Senators Eagleton of Missouri, Dole of Kansas, and Stevens of Alaska have recently sponsored legislation aimed at eliminating this undesirable feature. Under their "Federal System Plan", a President would be elected if the candidate won (1) a plurality of the national popular vote; and (2) either pluralities in more than 50% of the states and the District of Columbia, or pluralities in states with 50% of the voters in the election. If no candidate was elected, than all of a state's electoral votes automatically would be credited to the candidate who won a popular plurality in that state (thus eliminating the problem of the "faithless elector"). Under this plan a majority of the electoral votes (as now) would be sufficient for election. If still no candidate emerged victorious under the Electoral College formula, the electoral votes of third-party candidates would be automatically divided between the two leading candidates in proportion to their share of these states' popular vote.

Several other plans have been advocated throughout American history. The "District Plan", first introduced at the Constitutional Convention and later revived as the Mundt-Coudert plan after World War II, calls for the selection of Presidential electors according to election districts created by the state legislature. Following the pattern set for members of the Senate and House of Representatives, one electoral vote would go to the plurality winner in each district with two "at large" votes allocated to the candidate who captures a plurality of the state vote.

Such a plan would more accurately reflect the popular will by largely eliminating the "winner-take-all" feature of the present system. But it would put state legislatures in the position of apportioning the Presidential voting districts, a tremendous incentive to political shenanigans. For example, if states were not bound to use federal congressional districts, quadrennial gerrymandering and other kinds of political abuse conceivably could affect the way in which the President is elected.

The "Proportional Plan", first introduced in Congress in 1877 and periodically reconsidered, would leave the Electoral College intact but eliminate the office of Presidential elector. In brief, the plan calls for each candidate to receive the number of electoral votes in the state proportional to the popular vote received, thus eliminating the "general ticket" system. If no one received a majority of electoral votes, a runoff between the two top contenders would be held in a joint meeting of the House and Senate, with each member having one vote.

The variagated and complex ideas offered to correct the inadequacies in the Electoral College point up how difficult it is to achieve a satisfactory solution. But the effort should continue. The emergence of third party movements, symptomatic of political unrest in our constantly changing society, make drastic overhaul, or elimination, of the Electoral College an urgent item on the election reform timetable. The insistence on such reform demonstrates the growing equation of the individual's voting power with the maintenance of a stable political system and achieving genuine social change. And above all, a more equitable exercise of the right of franchise.

Campaign Expenditures and Corrupt Practices

As political analysts repeatedly affirm, and the public now generally concurs, present-day electioneering in the United

States is big business. It takes a wealthy person or a candidate with rich supporters to conduct an effective national campaign. Although the statement, "victory to the richest", is roundly condemned as an affront to democratic electoral principles, including the individual voter's right of choice, in practice, unfortunately, the assertion is wholly accurate. According to reported figures on national campaign costs, expenditures in the 1968 Presidential and Congressional elections totalled just below $70,000,000*, more than twice as much as spent in 1960. The table (p. 112), prepared by Congressional Quarterly, Inc., traces the soaring costs of campaigning in Presidential election years.

The fantastic rise of electronic media as the most puissant campaign tool is revealed in the figure of $49,300,000 spent in 1968 for radio and television broadcasts. These figures are more accurate than the total national campaign costs, due to the "built in" check on broadcasting expenditures that can be made by comparison with tax records. With this method of political campaigning reaching peak proportions, television campaigning cost the Democrats $14.4 million and the Republicans $13.5 million. Radio advertising accounted for almost $19 million, broken down into $10.8 million for the Democrats and $8.9 million for the Republicans. The chart (see p. 113), prepared by the Federal Communication Commission, gives a state-by-state breakdown of 1968 broadcast spending.

But long before the present-day concern over mounting costs, excessive political expenditures had prompted governmental intervention into campaign practices and spending at the federal and state levels. The 1925 Federal Corrupt Practices Act superceded a 1910 federal statute purporting to exercise at least minimal supervision over the campaign financing of political parties. The 1925 law essentially provided for the recording of all contributions and expenditures (over $10) by the treasurer of a political committee, and placed certain restraints on campaign giving and spending. For example, a limit was imposed on the amount that federal congressional candidates could spend in elections, $25,000 for a Senator and $5,000 for a Representative. The Act also made it unlawful for a candidate to promise political appointments in return for election support, and forbid the use of any expenditure to influence a person's vote. Campaign contributions by national banks or other corporations (later amended to include labor organizations), were forbidden.

---

*These are reported figures only and thus represent only a minimum amount. Because there are devices for funnelling unreported funds to candidates, there is no way of accurately estimating the true amount spent on political campaigns.

Financial temptation is no stranger to politics and lobbyists for special interest groups are skilled in the tactics of awarding special favors. Since quite often these practices can have an important effect on the election process (flying candidates in company planes, going special research, etc.), a new section was added to the federal statute in 1948 designed to curb abuses. Entitled the "Federal Regulation of Lobbying Act", this law restricted lobbyists' contributions and expenditures and provided for the reporting of all contributions over $500 by any individual who receives money for the purpose of influencing federal legislation.

While the Act set no limit on the amount a pressure group could contribute, it sought to regulate the purposes for which the money was spent. Promises of "support" for a cooperating legislator, lavish parties and gifts, or, occasionally, outright bribery are among the practices which the 1949 Act aimed to discourage by checking on lobbyists' receipts and expenditures.

As affluence and inflation soared side by side in the postwar era, and the cost of political campaigning grew correspondingly, the money factor became a key issue in practically all elections. Wealthy contributors were wooed by hard-pressed candidates and parties, often themselves ending up as party standard bearers. A general consensus developed that the financial emphasis could very seriously affect the purity of the election process. Different plans were proposed to try to reduce costs or control expenditures, by financing campaigns from the public treasury, chiefly through tax deductions to citizens who contributed to the party of their choice, and by forced disclosure of funding.

A final compromise, the 1971 Federal Election Campaign Act, sought to curb spending by placing absolute limits on certain contributions and expenditures and requiring disclosure. An ambitious attempt to regulate campaign spending, the Act covers Presidential and Congressional candidates. It limits outlays by candidates for federal office in any general, primary, or special election to 10¢ per constitutent, not more than 6¢ of which, (60% of the total) may be spent in any one media.

A specific limit of $8.4 million is imposed on how much Presidential candidates can spend on TV and radio during the post-convention campaign. For the first time, limits are placed on how much personal funds a candidate can spend in the campaign. Presidential and Vice-Presidential candidates are restricted to $50,000; Senate candidates to $35,000 and House candidates to $25,000. Disclosure provisions of the Act require candidates and political committees receiving and spending more than $1,000 to report all contributions and expenditures over $100.

Reports must be filed with the Congressional clerks or state officials three times a year (six times a year in election years).

The 1971 act is no panacea. Questions still remain about the fair allocation of radio-TV time, under the equal time provision of the federal communications law, and subterfuges have always been found to circumvent any campaign expense law. But at least a start has been made to curb the insidious effect of money on the election process.

The federal statute books contain other laws designed to preserve the sanctity of the voting system. One of these, the 1940 Hatch Act, is aimed at precluding government employees from exercising any improper influence in elections. Specifically, the Act forbids employees of federal, state or territorial governments from using their "official authority" to influence the outcome of a primary or general election. The U.S Supreme Court in the 1947 United Public Workers of America v. Mitchell case held these provisions of the Act constitutional on the broad ground that Congress possessed the power "within reasonable limits, to regulate, so far as it might deem necessary, the political conduct of its employees."

Since its passage, the Hatch Act has spawned considerable controversy. On the one hand, while government employment is predicated basically on merit, many employees hold positions with enormous potential for wrongful pressure on voters; the preservation of a non-partisan civil service makes the Act desirable. On the other hand, the Act's overbreadth and implementation (like dismissing a Texas postal carrier for writing a letter to a newspaper criticizing a candidate) has been attacked for denying freedom of speech. Its provisions, which embrace virtually any government employee, no matter how minor the position (only teachers are exempt), have prompted many election reform advocates to urge a more sensible approach, such as restricting political activity only to government employees in truly high-echelon positions. As the federal government's work force now tops 3 million, a compelling case can be made that the Act's all-inclusive coverage infringes the political action of a sizeable number of citizens. This point is being emphasized in new legal challenges now in the courts seeking to reverse the 1947 Mitchell decision.

The Hatch Act's federal proscription on who may influence an election is supplemented by laws regulating what types of activities are forbidden. In addition to the prohibition on expenditures to influence voting*, any person who uses Congressional

---

*Federal law also prohibits any contributions by agents of foreign principals, thus insuring that no foreign government can affect the outcome of an election.

appropriations (such as work relief, public works projects, or government loans or grants) for the purpose of coercing or interfering with the right to vote faces a $1,000 fine and a year's imprisonment.

The protective shield thrown over the election process covers material published in the campaign. A federal law requires persons or groups who publish or distribute political pamphlets or other writing to print their name (or the name of the organization) in the publication. Civil liberties exponents have assailed this provision as an infringement of free speech because forced disclosure may intimidate groups, especially those considered politically obnoxious, from publishing campaign literature; or prejudice the candidate because the public focus is on the source of the publication rather than the ideas and information it contains. But persons equally concerned with the civil liberties value of the public's "right to know" argue that in an election voters especially are entitled to know the source of a candidate's support so they may evaluate this information in determining for which candidate to vote. Moreover, required identification of the source is a safeguard against last-minute trickery to influence voters against a candidate by publishing material without the candidate's consent.

The Supreme Court has never passed on the precise question of laws prohibiting anonymity in election circulars, but in the 1960 Talley v. California case, the high court did invalidate a Los Angeles ordinance which made it unlawful to distribute "any hand-bill in any place under any circumstances" without revealing the author or sponsor. The Court ruled such a statute an unconstitutional abridgement of the right of free speech, noting that "an identification requirement would tend to restrict freedom to distribute information and thereby freedom of expression." When a narrower statute barring anonymous leaflets in election campaigns came before the Court in the 1969 Golden v. Zwickler case, the high tribunal declined to pass on the question, on the ground that the issue had become moot with the end of the election.

Because federal statutes refer mainly to federal elections only, or because they are not deemed strict enough, 45 of the 50 states (all states except Alaska, Delaware, Nevada, Pennsylvania, and Rhode Island) now have corrupt practices laws limiting to some extent campaign contributions to or expenditures by political candidates. In 41 of the 45 states (all except Idaho, Mississippi, Vermont and Washington), the laws apply to primary as well as general elections.

Varying widely with respect to who is covered by the laws and how much a candidate can spend on a campaign, the state codes reflect both a sincere attempt at regulation and ingenious approaches which offer little or no protection from campaign spending abuses. Of the 45 states limiting expenditures, Georgia, Illinois, Louisiana and North Dakota do not require the filing of financial statements, thus making enforcement all but impossible. Only 25 of these 45 states (Alabama, Arizona, Idaho, Indiana, Iowa, Kansas, Maryland, Massachusetts, Michigan, Minnesota, Missouri, Montana, New Hampshire, New Jersey, New York, North Dakota, Ohio, Oregon, South Dakota, Vermont, Virginia, West Virginia, Wisconsin, Wyoming, Mississippi) limit total costs by candidates, often exempting such expenditures as traveling, or the printing of written material. For example, Alabama exempts newspaper, television, and radio advertising expenses. Of the 25 states, however, only 13 (Indiana, Maryland, Michigan, Mississippi, New Hampshire, New York, North Dakota, Oklahoma, South Dakota, Texas, Vermont, West Virginia, Wyoming) also limit the amount that can be spent in behalf of the candidate,thus limiting the total amount able to be spent during the campaign.

In 30 states contributions by corporations are expressly prohibited. Oregon's statute applies solely to certain corporations, while only insurance companies are barred from contributing in Illinois. New Jersey prohibits exclusively insurance companies, public utilities, and banks. Additionally, three states, Indiana, New Hampshire and Texas, also prohibit political contributions from labor unions.

Financial corruption is only one of several electoral abuses that state laws aim to prevent. In addition to the Corrupt Practices Acts, separate laws make criminally punishable a comprehensive set of election offenses that cover election officials in the performance of official duties, voters as individual citizens, political parties' activities, and candidates in the conduct of campaigns.

The most universally condemned activities are bribery or other unlawful solicitation of votes, or intimidation or hinderance of an elector. Penalties for committing such crimes vary among the states, with the most frequent sanction being disfranchisement for periods ranging from two years to life. An equally serious election offense is betting on the outcome of an election, a practice specifically prohibited in 41 states. The offense of perjury committed in connection with affidavits or oaths which an elector takes attesting to the accuracy of his or her statements, is punishable by fine and imprisonment, as is fraud connected with registration or actual voting.

In most states, the public official who tampers with an electoral procedure faces more severe punishment than disfranchisement. For example, in Virginia, corrupt conduct by any election officer in the execution of duties is a felony punishable by a $1,000 fine and imprisonment for up to one year. California also brands corrupt election officers as "felons".

Private employers in 36 states are prevented from attempting to coerce the political decisions of their employees. A New Jersey statute, for example, requires a corporation to forfeit its charter if a corporation official is found guilty of undue political pressure. A similar penalty exists in Tennessee, Rhode Island, and other states. Rhode Island's law additionally provides that any attempt by an employer to intimidate employees in voting results in the loss of that employer's voting privileges.

The chart, p. 114, taken from "Election Law Guidebook, 1970", a publication of the U.S. Government Printing Office, lists the specific election offenses declared unlawful by the states.

Obstacles for New, Minority Parties

Under an ideal election system, the people are entitled to vote for those candidates who they believe best represent their interests. This principle, coupled with the First Amendment's guarantee of free association and free speech, includes the right of new political parties to be born and seek popular support. Citizens have different ideas as to the policies and programs that government should adopt, and if such beliefs are shared by a substantial number of people, there should be a way to express these opinions at the polls.

These premises, the underpinning of democratic government, become less viable if the electorate is not given the chance to choose among candidates that represent a real cross-section of political views. Because the major parties, as huge conglomerates of public opinion, must cater to a broad spectrum of the electorate, their candidates are pressed not to suggest too radical, innovative political programs. Yet, unless voters with dissident political views find some way to effectuate their beliefs by supporting new parties, it can be argued that segments of the electorate are effectively disfranchised.

A truly open political system places on the predominant political parties the responsibility voluntarily to ease restrictions facing independent candidates and new parties. Yet the

94

Democratic and Republican parties, understandably reluctant to relinquish their own political power, have written the legislative rules so as to impede the organization of third parties. Predictably, reform has been slow, led in large measure by court decisions voiding restrictive state laws.

Interestingly, no state bans in principle the organization of new parties. But numerous and often subtle obstacles are placed in the path of independent parties and candidates. These restrictions center on denying access to the ballot to certain individuals or political groups or by demanding something "extra", such as a nominating petition or filing fee.

States justify such steps on the grounds that minor parties do not reflect the popular will and those parties that do (usually measured by the number of votes received at a previous election) deserve favored treatment. The expense involved in administering an election where every political grouping is on the ballot is also noted. Behind these arguments lies the long-standing theory that America's extraordinary political stability is directly linked to a two-party system which places a premium on political compromise. In the opinion of political scientists, precisely because of this system, the United States has avoided the constant changes of government and political instability which are the hallmark of nations with multi-party systems, such as Italy and France. The laws and court decisions mirror these contentions and the delicate balance the legislatures and judiciary have tried to strike between the freedoms due political dissidents and the perceived needs of an orderly political system.

The desire for stability and fear of drastic political change underlie the prohibition that all state laws contain, a provision that no political party or candidate advocating the violent overthrow of the United States Government can appear on the ballot. Fifteen states (Alabama, Arizona, Arkansas, Florida, Illinois, Kansas, Louisiana, Mississippi, Nebraska, Oklahoma, Pennsylvania, Texas, Washington, Wisconsin and Wyoming) seek even more security by specifically excluding the Communist Party from electoral participation. These statutes, largely a hangover from the post-World War II era, when anti-Communist sentiment ran high among the American people, offer false security and blatantly offend constitutional principles. They have been properly criticized by civil liberties experts on the grounds that all political opinions, no matter how unpopular, should compete in the electoral market-place.

Because the "Communist menace" is so poorly defined, the statutes are often couched in vague, overly broad language which can exclude legitimate political contenders. Illinois' law, for example, states

> that no political organization or group shall be qualified as a political party hereunder, or given a place on the ballot, which organization or group is associated, directly or indirectly, with Communist, Fascist, Nazi, or other un-American principles and engages in activities or propaganda designed to teach subservience to the political principles and ideals of foreign nations or the overthrow by violence of the established constitutional form of government of the United States and the State of Illinois.

The statute's obscure language makes it extremely difficult for some political parties to determine whether they fall within the prohibition. What is "un-American"? What constitutes teaching "subservience to the political principles and ideals of foreign nations"? Is a political party which advocates Britain's parliamentary system of government forbidden a place on the ballot? These and related questions call into question the usefullness and legitimacy of such statutes.

A second form of state prejudice against minor parties or independent candidates is discriminatory petition or filing requirements designed to discourage the formation of third parties. Republicans and Democrats often face no procedural obstacles in gaining access to the ballot or in participating in primary elections. In most states, major party candidates are assigned a place on the ballot by virtue of a primary victory or a simple filing of a "Declaration of Candidacy". But for an independent candidate to win a ballot spot, he or she must first submit to the appropriate state official, usually the Secretary of State, a petition signed by a specified number of voters.

The petition requirements for minor parties are defended on the bases that they are a reasonable exercise of state authority over the election process, and that some screening procedure is justified to guard against spurious challenges by less than serious contenders. While these arguments appear sound, they do not overcome the serious constitutional questions arising from state petition requirements which exceed all bounds of reasonable regulation.

The state-by-state petition requirements vary widely. Most follow a reasonable pattern, 1% or 2% of the gubernatorial vote cast for statewide candidates in the preceding election. But a few pose formidable hurdles, such as North Carolina's proviso that petition signatures for a Congressional candidate number 25% of the gubernatorial vote in the Congressional district.

Some states lessen the impact of their requirements by placing an absolute limit on the requisite number of signatures. For example, in North Dakota, independent candidates for United States Representative must file petitions totalling 10% of the votes cast in the last election for United States Representative, but these need not exceed 300 signatures. Similar requirements for Congressional candidates exist in New Jersey (2% but not to exceed 100); Nebraska (10% of district vote for Governor but not to exceed 1,000); New York (5% of gubernatorial district votes but not to exceed 3,000 from any one county, or, if in New York City, not to exceed 3,000); and Minnesota (5% of the district vote at the last election or 1,000, whichever is less).

Generally, the courts have upheld reasonable petition provisions, but some judges have struck down requirements that are so burdensome that they bear no rational relation to their ostensible purpose, protection of the ballot from spurious challenges and the easing of administrative burdens. In the 1968 Williams v. Rhodes case, the Supreme Court voided an Ohio petition requirement which was part of a comprehensive scheme designed to discourage the emergence of independent parties. The Ohio law required that before the Presidential candidate of an independent party could appear on the ballot, the party had to obtain signatures equal to 15% of the votes cast in the preceding gubernatorial election--an all but impossible task in view of the necessary 435,100 signatures.

The Court ruled such a prohibitive requirement an unconstitutional violation of the 14th Amendment's equal protection clause. As Justice Hugo Black declared:

No extended discussion is required to establish that the Ohio laws before us give the two-established parties a decided advantage over any new parties struggling for existence and thus place substantially unequal burdens on both the right to vote and the right to associate. The right to form a party for the advancement of political goals means little if a party can be kept off the election ballot and thus denied an equal opportunity to win votes. So also, the right to vote is heavily burdened if that vote may be cast only for one of two parties at a time when other parties are clamoring for a place on the ballot.

Other constitutional doctrines have been invoked to invalidate unfair petitional requirements. In the 1969 Moore v. Ogilvie case, the Supreme Court invalidated an Illinois law requiring that nominating petitions for independent candidates be signed by at least 25,000 persons, including 200 from each of at least 50 of the state's 102 counties. The Court reasoned that because the counties were unequally populated (93.4% of Illinois' registered voters lived in the 49 most populous counties. 6.6% resided in the remaining 53 counties), the statute violated the one-person, one-vote rule by effectively granting more weight to the signatures of voters in sparsely populated rural counties than to voters' signatures in densely populated urban counties.

A reasonable time period to collect petitional signatures comes within constitutional boundaries. In 1972, the Supreme Court upheld Georgia's law allowing 180 days to collect the signatures of 5% of the persons eligible to vote for the office the candidate is seeking. However, a mere three-week period to collect names is under attack in a Pennsylvania case involving that state's requirement that the signatures total 2% of the largest vote cast for any state-wide candidate in the previous election (for the 1972 election, 35,624 signatures are necessary).

Several states, among them California, Texas and Washington, utilize another petitional device to impede new parties. They stipulate that signers must not have voted at another party's primary election. This can be a severe hurdle for a party to overcome because it narrows the class of potential signers to those few voters who are politically interested enough to sign an independent candidate's petition, but who were not sufficiently motivated to vote in a party primary.

Financial restrictions have been created to discourage independent parties or candidates, usually in the form of a filing fee or other assessment connected with a primary election. The filing fee is applied uniformly to major party or independent candidates for a particular office. But the heavily financed major parties have a distinct advantage as they usually have no trouble paying the fee. Furthermore, several states provide for return of the fee upon a polling of a certain percentage of the total vote-- another clear benefit to the major party candidates.

The fees are sometimes set at a percentage of the salary of the office sought. Alabama and Virginia do not exceed 2% of one year's salary. California, Kansas, Montana, Nebraska, North Carolina, Washington and West Virginia take only 1% of the first year's salary; Connecticut's fee is 5% of the annual salary. Florida's is 3% of the annual salary. Ohio's is 1/2 of 1% of the annual salary but not more than $50. Utah's is 1/4 of 1% of the total salary for the full term.

Other states establish absolute dollar amounts. Not more than $200 (Mississippi); $200 (Oklahoma); $150 (Nevada); $100 (Alaska, Louisiana, Maryland, Minnesota, Oregon); $75 (Hawaii); $50 (Missouri, New Hampshire); $35 (Pennsylvania); $20 (Wyoming); $10 (Arkansas plus "ballot fees" in the amount required by the party).

Three states, Georgia, South Carolina and Texas, provide open-ended requirements. Georgia requires independent candidates to pay "reasonable" qualifying fees as determined by the Secretary of State. South Carolina's primary filing fee is fixed by the state executive committee of the party. In Texas, the party committee estimates the cost of the primary and then apportions it among candidates according to what, in its judgment, is "just and equitable", in light of "the importance, emolument, and term of office."

Following in the vein of their petitional requirement decisions, the courts generally have upheld a state's power to impose reasonable filing fees on primary or other candidates. A recent Supreme Court decision, however, indicated that these requirements, too, must conform to equal protection standards. In the 1972 Bullock v. Carter case, the high court struck down Texas' primary filing fee requirement. The Court noted that the fee, which ranged as high as $8,900 in some elections, effectively precluded poor candidates from the ballot. This was constitutionally prohibited, the Court said, in light of the fact that, under Texas law, no alternative means of appearing on the primary ballot existed. (In Texas, no write-ins are allowed in primaries. Further, no petition procedure exists).

The over-all conclusion that can be drawn with respect to independent candidates or minor parties is that the states, subject to constitutional limitations of equal protection, have broad power to regulate their parties' access to the ballot. The courts will intervene only when a particular requirement really deters political participation.

No one can quarrel with the need for state regulation to assure sensible election procedures, but the present discriminatory restrictions should be ended so minor parties and independent candidates can have the best opportunity to present their views to the voters. We should remember that our pluralistic society can realize its potential only by the infusion of fresh insight and new plans for redressing social grievances. Some of the benefits now taken for granted, such as women's suffrage, Social Security, or medicare, were ideas voiced by yesterday's "radicals" who pursued their goals through the voting process. Even though not victorious at the polls, their candidacy served an indispensible educational role in opening the eyes of the major parties--and the nation--to how certain social ills could be relieved.

Residence Requirements for the 50 States *

	State	County	District, Precinct, or Ward	City or Town
Ala.	1 yr.	6 mos.	3 mos.	
Alaska	1 yr.		30 days	
Ariz.	1 yr.	30 days	30 days	
Ark.	1 yr.	6 mos.	30 days	
Calif.	90 days	90 days	54 days	
Colo.	3 mos.		29 days	
Conn.				6 mos.(town)
Del.	1 yr.	3 mos.	30 days	
Fla.	1 yr.	6 mos.		
Ga.	1 yr.	6 mos.		
Hawaii	1 yr.			
Idaho	6 mos.	30 days		
Ill.	6 mos.		30 days	
Ind.	6 mos.	60 days (town-ship)	30 days	
Iowa	6 mos.	60 days	10 days	
Kansas	6 mos.		30 days (ward or township)	
Ky.	1 yr.	6 mos.	60 days	
La.	1 yr.	6 mos.(parish)	3 mos.	
Me.	6 mos.			3 mos. (munici-pality)
Md.	6 mos.	28 days (county or city)		28 days (county or city)

* Taken from the state election codes.

Residence Requirements (cont.)

	State	County	District, Precinct, or Ward	City or Town
Mass.	1 yr.			6 mos.(city or town)
Mich.	6 mos.		must reside in city or township on or before the 5th Friday preceeding election	
*Minn.	30 days		30 days	
Miss.	1 yr.	1 yr.	6 mos.	
Mo.	1 yr.	60 days (county, city or town)		60 days (county, city or town)
Montana	1 yr.	30 days		
Neb.	6 mos.	40 days	10 days	
Nev.	6 mos.	30 days	10 days	
N.H.			6 mos.	
N.J.	6 mos.	40 days		
N.Mex.	1 yr.	90 days	30 days	
N.Y.	3 mos.	3 mos.(county, city or village)		3 mos.(county, city or village)
N.Car.	1 yr.		30 days	
N.Dak.	1 yr.	90 days	30 days	
Ohio	6 mos.	40 days	40 days	
Okla.	6 mos.	2 mos.	20 days	
Ore.	6 mos.			
**Pa.	90 days		60 days	
R.I.	1 yr.			6 mos.
S.Car.	6 mos.	3 mos.	30 days	
+ S.Dak.	180 days	90 days	30 days	
Tenn.	1 yr.	3 mos.		
‡ Texas	1 yr.	6 mos.		

	State	County	District Precinct, or Ward	City or Town
Utah	6 mos.	60 days		
Vt.	90 days			90 days (for Representatives to the General Assembly or for Justices)
Va.	6 mos.		30 days	
Wash.	1 yr.	90 days	30 days (city or voting precinct)	
W.Va.	1 yr.	60 days (county or municipality)		
Wis.	6 mos.		10 days	
Wyo.	1 yr.	60 days	10 days	

+ One year state resident may vote on statewide issues even though not fulfilling county residence requirement.

‡ U.S. resident for 5 years. Intercounty or interprecinct movers may vote in former residence until new voting residence is acquired.

* Interprecinct movers may still vote.

** Interdistrict movers who move within 60 days may vote in former district.

State Policies On
Student Voting in College Communities
(As of November 22, 1971)

Chart Key

1. Students are treated in exactly the same manner as all other
   voter applicants. So long as they meet the local durational
   residency requirements (e.g. 6 months in the state, 30 days
   in the county), they are allowed to register by merely
   declaring their intent to make the county their voting
   residence.

2. Students may vote in their college community though some
   minimal questioning to verify their intent may be conducted.

3. A student's voting residence is presumed to be his parents'
   community and this presumption cannot be overcome if a student
   lives in a dormitory, pays out-of-state tuition, or receives
   financial support from his parents.

4. Under no circumstance can students register in their college
   community. They must register where their parents live.

State	1	2	3	4
*Alabama			X	
Alaska	X			
Arizona		Not Clarified		
*Arkansas			X	
*California	X			
Colorado		X		
*Connecticut	X			
*Delaware			X	
Florida	X			
Georgia	X			

State	1	2	3	4
Hawaii				X
Idaho	X			
*Illinois	X			
*Indiana				X[1]
Iowa			X	
Kansas	X			
*Kentucky			X	
*Louisiana	X			
*Maine				X
*Maryland		X		
*Massachusetts	X			
*Michigan	X			
Minnesota			X	
*Mississippi				X
Missouri	X			
Montana				X[2]
Nebraska	X			
Nevada	X			
*New Hampshire				X
*New Jersey			X[3]	
New Mexico		X		

State	1	2	3	4
*New York				X
*North Carolina				X
*North Dakota			X	
*Ohio			X[4]	
Oklahoma	X			
Oregon	X			
*Pennsylvania	X			
Rhode Island	X			
*South Carolina				X
*South Dakota	X			
*Tennessee				X
*Texas				X
Utah		X		
Vermont			X	
*Virginia			X	
Washington	X			
West Virginia	X			
Wisconsin	X			
*Wyoming		X		

(1) #1, however, as to Delaware County
(2) as to unemancipated 18 year olds only; otherwise #1
(3) #1, however, as to Mercer County
(4) #1, however, as to Hamilton County

---

* Student residency suit being planned or already filed.

Groups Included in Non-Civilian Absentee Voter Category

State	Members of Armed Forces while in active service	Members of Merchant Marine	Civilian Employees of United States serving outside territorial limits	Members of religious groups or welfare agencies serving with Armed Forces
	Including spouses and dependents when shown in parentheses (X)			
Alabama[1]	(X)			
Alaska	(X)	(X)	(X)	
Arizona	X	X		
Arkansas	(X)	(X)	(X)[2]	
California	(X)		(X)[2]	(X)
Colorado	(X)	(X)	(X)	(X)
Connecticut[3]	(X)		(X)	(X)
Delaware[4]	(X)	(X)		(X)
Florida	(X)	(X)	(X)	(X)
Georgia[5]	(X)	(X)	(X)[2]	(X)
Hawaii	(X)	(X)	(X)[2]	
Idaho	(X)	(X)	(X)	(X)
Illinois	(X)	(X)	(X)	(X)
Indiana	(X)	(X)		
Iowa	(X)	(X)	(X)	(X)
Kansas	(X)	(X)	(X)[2]	
Kentucky	(X)	(X)	(X)	(X)
Louisiana	(X)	(X)	(X)	(X)
Maine	(X)	(X)	(X)	(X)

Groups Included in Non-Civilian Absentee Voter Category (cont.)

Maryland	(X)	(X)	(X)	(X)[6]
Massachusetts[7]	(X)	(X)	(X)[?]	
Michigan[8]	(X)		(X)	
Minnesota	(X)	(X)	$(X)^2$	
Mississippi[9]	(X)	(X)		(X)
Missouri	(X)	(X)	(X)	(X)
Montana	(X)	(X)	$(X)^2$	(X)
Nebraska	(X)	(X)	$(X)^2$	
Nevada	(X)	(X)	(X)	(X)
New Hampshire	(X)	(X)	(X)	(X)
New Jersey[10]	(X)			(X)
New Mexico	(X)	(X)	$(X)^2$	
New York	(X)			
North Carolina	(X)	X		
North Dakota	(X)	(X)	(X)	(X)
Ohio	(X)			
Oklahoma	(X)	(X)		(X)
Oregon	X	X	X^2	
Pennsylvania[11]	(X)	(X)	(X)	(X)
Rhode Island	(X)	(X)		(X)
South Carolina	(X)	X	X	X^{12}
South Dakota[13]	(X)		(X)	(X)
Tennessee	(X)	(X)	(X)	(X)
Texas	(X)	(X)	$(X)^2$	
Utah	(X)	(X)	(X)	(X)
Vermont	(X)	(X)	(X)	(X)
Virginia	(X)[14]			

Washington[15]	(X)	(X)	(X)[2]	(X)
West Virginia	(X)	(X)	(X)	
Wisconsin	(X)	(X)	(X)	(X)
Wyoming	(X)	(X)	(X)	(X)

1. Also persons employed outside the U.S. and their spouses and dependents.

2. Includes any United States citizen temporarily residing outside of territorial United States.

3. Merchant Marine and spouses and dependents are permitted to register absentee.

4. Also, American Red Cross, Society of Friends, USO, or any other group accompanying or serving with the Armed Forces or Merchant Marine.

5. Includes any civilian employee of the United States, residing outside the state, and his spouse and dependents.

6. Includes, American Red Cross, Society of Friends, Women's Auxiliary Service Pilots, USO groups. Also included is any citizen or resident continuously absent from his county of resident (or, if a resident of Baltimore, continuously absent for 30 days from Baltimore City prior to the close of registration).

7. Also Peace Corps Members, Cadets of the Service Academies.

8. Also civilian employees of the Armed Forces.

9. Also includes disabled hospitalized war veterans, drivers, operators or crewmen employed in interstate common carrier transportation service.

10. Also reservists in training and patients in a veterans hospital located outside their place of residence.

11. Also veterans bedridden or hospitalized outside their county of residence.

12. American Red Cross and USO personnel only.

13. Also members of Environmental Science Services Administration, Public Health Service, and others, their spouses and dependents.

14. Includes military personnel and spouses only.

15. Also students and faculty of the United States Military Academies.

Urban and Rural Population of the United States: 1790 - 1970

United States	Total Population	Urban % of Total	Rural % of Total
Current urban definition:			
1970	203,211,926	73.5	26.5
1960	179,323,175	69.9	30.1
1950	151,325,798	64.0	36.0
Previous urban definition:			
1960	179,323,175	63.0	37.0
1950	151,325,798	59.6	40.4
1940	132,164,569	56.5	43.5
1930	123,202,624	56.1	43.9
1920	106,021,537	51.2	48.8
1910	92,228,496	45.6	54.4
1900	76,212,168	39.6	60.4
1890	62,979,766	35.1	64.9
1880	50,189,209	28.2	71.8
1870	38,558,371	25.7	74.3
1860	31,443,321	19.8	80.2
1850	23,191,876	15.3	84.7
1840	17,069,453	10.8	89.2
1830	12,866,020	8.8	91.2
1820	9,638,453	7.2	92.8
1810	7,239,881	7.3	92.7
1800	5,308,483	6.1	93.9
1790	3,929,214	5.1	94.9

PRESIDENTIAL ELECTION, 1960 - BREAKDOWN OF VOTES

	Kennedy (D)	Nixon (R)	Others	Total Vote
Popular vote	34,227,096	34,108,546	502,363	68,838,005
% of Total	49.7	49.5	0.7	100
Electoral vote	303	219	15	537
% of Total	56.4	40.8	2.8	100

PRESIDENTIAL ELECTION, 1968 - BREAKDOWN OF VOTES

	Nixon (R)	Humphrey (D)	Wallace (I)	Others	Total Vote
Popular vote	31,785,480	31,275,166	9,906,473	243,044	73,210,163
% of Total	43.4	42.7	13.5	0.3	100
Electoral vote	301	191	46	0	538
% of Total *	55.9	35.5	8.6	0	100

* Any variances due to rounding.

<u>Election Campaign Costs for National Offices: 1960 to 1968</u>

<u>Money figures in thousands of dollars</u>. Covers expenditures
officially reported to the Clerk of the House and the Secretary
of the Senate. Cost of political activities at all levels,
including primaries and intrastate committees, estimated by
Citizens' Research Foundation at $200 million for 1964 and $300
million for 1968. Known campaign debts not actually reported
are added to reported expenditures to determine total spending.

Item	1960	1964	1968[1]
Campaign costs	<u>32,896</u>	<u>47,763</u>	<u>69,999</u>
National spending	28,074	38,601	62,765
Expenditures reported	23,504	37,401	61,765
Debt	4,570	1,200	1,000
Congressional spending	4,822	9,162	8,483
Democratic	2,250	5,736	4,974
Republican	2,524	3,369	3,184
Third Party	48	58	325
(Less Lateral Transfers)	--	—	(1,249)
Democratic Committees:			
Number reporting	29	49	97
Spending	11,801	13,349	13,578
Percent of national spending	42.0	34.6	21.6
Expenditures	7,981	12,149	12,578
1Debt	3,820	1,200	1,000[2]
Republican Committees:			
Number reporting	43	41	46
Spending	12,950	19,315	29,443
Percent of national spending	46.1	50.0	46.9
Expenditures	12,200	19,315	29,443
Debt	750	-	-
Wallace campaign:			
Spending	X	X	7,243
Percent of national spending	X	X	11.5
Labor committees:			
Number reporting	60	40	46
Expenditures	2,451	3,816	7,632
Percent of national spending	8.7	9.9	12.2
Miscellaneious committees:			
Number reporting	22	34	66
Spending	873	2,121	4,869
Percent of national spending	3.1	5.5	7.8

- Represents zero. X means not applicable.

1. Later fund transfers between national level committees have
been deducted from expenditures and receipts except for the labor
and miscellaneous committees expenditures, which represent total
reported spending, even when some of the funds were transferred
to other committees. The lateral transfers by labor committees,
$1,305,000 and by miscellaneous groups, $214,000, are subtracted
to avoid counting them twice in total "campaign costs".

2. Democratic National Committee debt: Covers only unpaid post-
convention presidential campaign expenses; excludes some $5 million
in unpaid loans.

Expenditures for Political Broadcasts for Elections, By Medium and Party: 1968

In thousands of dollars, except as indicated. Represents media charges for primary and general elections.

State	Total[1] Amount	Total[1] Per Potential voter[2]	Radio R	Radio D	Television R	Television D
U.S.	49,315	0.42	8,658	10,303	13,507	14,373
Alabama	453	.22	33	178	41	163
Alaska	356	2.89	64	83	91	108
Arizona	448	.48	68	148	97	117
Arkansas	986	.84	221	230	205	296
California	5,031	.43	624	1,092	1,373	1,646
Colorado	351	.30	83	67	116	70
Connecticut	334	.18	67	95	59	94
Delaware	97	.32	72	22	-	-
D.C.	427	.86	24	42	151	182
Florida	2,335	.62	411	614	577	654
Georgia	867	.31	80	314	157	268
Hawaii	555	1.48	85	126	149	192
Idaho	142	.36	35	27	38	34
Illinois	2,765	.42	437	393	1,096	772
Indiana	1,608	.54	265	309	352	626
Iowa	772	.47	175	115	247	223
Kansas	589	.44	128	118	187	148
Kentucky	412	.20	64	82	84	162
Louisiana	884	.44	37	166	151	491
Maine	170	.30	35	26	57	50
Maryland	467	.22	83	116	115	91
Massachusetts	600	.18	78	144	181	138
Michigan	1,144	.23	260	162	310	201
Minnesota	447	.21	77	71	115	123
Mississippi	63	.05	3	17	4	22
Missouri	2,420	.87	299	514	686	865
Montana	317	.80	68	71	74	92
Nebraska	315	.37	42	51	73	112
Nevada	361	1.31	29	33	109	136
New Hampshire	161	.38	59	75	16	7
New Jersey	238	.05	106	99	11	5
New Mexico	313	.60	59	110	50	91
New York	3,874	.33	544	455	1,544	1,195
N. Carolina	1,125	.39	149	284	247	398
N. Dakota	305	.85	50	27	106	93
Ohio	2,731	.44	888	334	882	471
Oklahoma	670	.45	83	147	184	219
Oregon	1,190	.96	154	218	393	334
Pennsylvania	2,120	.29	376	258	889	476
Rhode Island	414	.76	48	87	141	126
S. Carolina	601	.43	92	184	121	172
S. Dakota	223	.58	36	56	49	75
Tennessee	1,747	.74	1,003	146	243	270
Texas	3,576	.58	456	850	779	1,344
Utah	253	.46	38	41	60	107
Vermont	69	.28	23	15	21	9
Virginia	299	.12	59	42	96	70
Washington	675	.38	128	186	139	187
W. Virginia	661	.61	150	153	173	151
Wisconsin	2,281	.92	189	1,097	443	487
Wyoming	73	.40	22	14	26	6

- Represents zero.

1. Includes other parties not shown seperately.

2. Based on civilian residents of voting age as of November 1, 1968 as estimated by the Bureau of the Census.

ELECTION OFFENSES

State	Unlawful solicitation of votes, corruptly influencing voter, bribery	Intimidation of or hindering voter	Gift or promise of money or thing of value to person to vote or not to vote	Entertainment to promote an election	Transportation of voters	Intoxicating liquor, furnishing on election day, etc.	Bribing members of a political nominating meeting	Betting on outcome of election	Unidentified advertising and other printed matter	Solicitation of funds from candidate by certain organizations and persons	Failure to file statement of campaign finances	Contributions by certain corporations or labor unions	Election coercion by employer	Tampering with voting machine, ballot box	Electioneering near polls	Payment for withdrawal of candidate	Time off for voting, failure to give	Contributions under fictitious names	Use of appropriated funds to influence election	See pt. II for other offenses
Alabama	X	X	X	X	X	X		X	X	X	X	X	X							X
Alaska	X	X	X		X		X	X	X		X	X	X	X	X		X			X
Arizona	X	X	X			X	X	X	X		X	X	X	X	X					X
Arkansas	X	X	X	X		X	X	X	X		X	X	X		X		X			X
California	X	X	X			X		X	X	X	X	X	X	X	X	X	X	X		X
Colorado	X	X	X			X		X	X		X	X	X	X	X	X	X			X
Connecticut	X	X	X			X	X	X	X		X	X	X	X	X	X	X			X
Delaware	X	X	X						X			X								X
Florida	X	X						X	X	X	X									X
Georgia	X	X	X						X						X	X				X
Hawaii	X	X	X	X		X	X	X	X	X	X	X		X	X			X		X
Idaho	X	X	X			X		X	X		X	X	X	X	X		X		X	X
Illinois	X	X	X		X	X	X	X	X	X	X	X	X	X	X	X	X			X
Indiana	X	X	X	X		X		X	X		X	X	X		X		X			X
Iowa	X	X	X	X		X	X	X	X	X	X	X	X	X	X		X			X
Kansas	X	X	X			X		X	X									X		X
Kentucky	X	X	X			X		X	X		X									X
Louisiana	X	X	X			X		X	X	X	X									X
Maine	X	X	X			X		X	X	X	X			X	X		X	X		X

114

State													
Maryland	X	X	X	X		X	X	X	X		X	X		X
Massachusetts	X	X	X	X		X	X	X	X	X	X	X	X	X
Michigan	X	X	X	X		X	X	X	X	X	X	X	X	X
Minnesota	X		X			X	X	X	X	X	X			X
Mississippi	X	X	X	X		X	X	X	X	X	X	X		X
Missouri	X		X	X¹		X	X	X	X	X	X	X	X	X
Montana	X		X	X¹		X	X	X	X	X	X	X		X
Nebraska	X		X	X		X	X	X	X		X	X		X
Nevada	X		X	X		X	X	X	X	X	X	X		X
New Hampshire	X	X	X	X		X	X	X	X	X	X	X	X	X
New Jersey	X	X	X	X		X	X	X	X	X	X	X		X
New Mexico	X		X	X		X	X	X	X		X	X	X	X
New York	X		X	X¹		X	X	X	X	X	X	X	X	X
North Carolina	X	X	X	X¹	X	X	X	X	X		X	X		X
North Dakota	X	X	X	X	X	X	X	X	X	X	X	X		X
Ohio	X	X	X	X		X	X	X	X	X	X	X	X	X
Oklahoma	X	X	X	X		X	X	X	X	X	X	X	X	X
Oregon	X		X	X		X	X	X	X	X	X	X		X
Pennsylvania	X		X	X		X	X	X	X	X	X	X	X	X
Rhode Island	X		X	X		X	X	X	X	X	X	X	X	X
South Carolina	X		X	X		X	X	X	X		X	X		X
South Dakota	X		X	X		X	X	X	X		X	X		X
Tennessee	X	X	X	X¹		X	X	X	X	X	X	X	X	X
Texas	X	X	X	X¹		X	X	X	X	X	X	X	X	X
Utah	X	X	X	X¹		X	X	X	X	X	X	X		X
Vermont	X		X	X	X	X	X	X	X		X	X		X
Virginia	X		X	X¹		X	X	X	X	X	X	X	X	X
Washington	X		X	X		X	X	X	X		X	X		X
West Virginia	X	X	X	X¹		X	X	X	X		X	X	X	X
Wisconsin	X	X	X	X	X	X	X	X	X		X	X		X
Wyoming	X		X	X		X	X	X	X	X	X	X		X

¹ Except the sick and infirm.

State Registration Requirements

STATE	WHEN MAY YOU REGISTER?	WHAT OFFICIAL DO YOU SEE?	WHAT CIVILIAN VOTERS MAY REGISTER ABSENTEE?	HOW IS ABSENTEE REGISTRATION ACCOMPLISHED?
Alabama	In odd numbered years, board of registrar of each county meets at least once between Oct. 1st and Dec. 31st in each precinct. In even numbered years, board meets for at least 10 working days beginning the 3rd Monday in January. Additional sessions may be held. Consult your local registrar. Books close 10 days before any election	Board of Registrars	No absentee registration	
Alaska *	Anytime up to 14 days preceding election (Anytime up to 30 days preceding election if application is by mail.	Any registration official	Anyone who believes he will be unavoidably absent from voting precinct on election day	Mail application postmarked at least 30 days prior to an election to Lieutenant Governor or appropriate registration official
Arizona *	Anytime up to 5 P.M. of day two months preceding a primary election; or anytime up to 5 P.M. of the 8th Monday preceding a general election. Re-registration required every 10 years.	Recorder of county or Deputy Registrar of Precinct.	Any elector temporarily absent from the State	Remit properly executed application obtained from county recorder

Registration Requirements (cont.)

Arkansas	Anytime except 20 days prior to any election. During the 20 days, registration for up-coming election shall cease, but voter may then register for subsequent elections	Permanent Registrar's Office	No absentee registration
California*	Anytime except during 53 days prior to election	County Clerk (Registrar of Voters in Los Angeles, San Francisco, San Diego, San Bernadino and Santa Clara).	Any elector absent from his county of residence	Execute Affidavit of Registration forms. Remit to County Clerk or Registrar of Voters. May also register in county other than county of residence.
Colorado *	Anytime after 45 days following a general election up to the 20th day before the primary election, or anytime after the primary election up to the 20th day before the general election.	County Clerk (Election Commission in Denver)	Voters absent from county during regis-tration period, or those seriously ill.	File a properly executed affidavit during registration period.
Connecticut *	Boards must meet at least once for 4 hours on Sat. of 4th or 6th week before regular election. Addition-al sessions are optional. Monthly sessions are also required. Consult your local board for details.	Board for the Admission of Electors	No absentee registration	

Registration Requirements (cont.)

Delaware *	In even-numbered years on 4th Sat. in July, and 3rd Sat. in Oct. Consult local Dept. of Elections for dates of additional sessions	Dept. of Elections	No absentee registration	
District of Columbia	Any time up to 30 days prior to election	Board of Elections	Any absent elector	Apply any time for official absentee registration form, Remit prior to close of registration
Florida	Anytime except 30 days prior and 5 days after any election	Supervisor of Registration	No absentee registration	
Georgia *	Anytime up to 50 days prior to a November election. Registration may also be suspended on the day a primary election is held.	County Registrar	No absentee registration	
Hawaii *	Anytime up to 45 days prior to a primary, special for general election, anytime up to midnight of the 5th day following the primary election.	County Clerk (City Clerk in Honolulu)	Any qualified elector	Obtain official application form from County Clerk (City Clerk in Honolulu). Complete executed form and remit during registration period.
Idaho *	Anytime up to 10 days preceding election at precinct registration, or anytime up to 2 days preceding election at office of the County Clerk.	County Clerk or official registrar	Any elector absent from the State	Mail request for registration to County Clerk, postmarked not less than 10 days before election. Remit properly executed registration card to County Clerk

118

Registration Requirements (cont.)

Illinois *	Where registration required, anytime except weekends and legal holidays up to 28 days preceding any election. Books reopen on 2nd day following an election.	Town, City, Village or County Clerk (in Chicago, Board of Election Commissioners)	Any qualified elector absent from place of residence due to government business, or electors outside U.S. territorial limits.	By mail to the Board of Election Commissioners during registration period.
Indiana *	From Dec. 1st of each year in which a general or city election is held up to the 29th day preceding the county or city primary. Books reopen on May 15th next succeeding the county or city primary and remains open until the 29th day before the general or city election. Deputy registrars close books 45 days prior to an election.	Clerk of Circuit Court (Board of Registration in Counties with over 80,000 registered voters)	Any qualified absent person	Request "Absentee Registration" form from appropriate official. (Clerk of Circuit Court, or office of Board of Registration). Remit executed form in time to reach officials no later than 29 days before election.
Iowa	Where registration required prior to election during designated registration times. Consult local officials.	City Clerk (Commissioner of Registration in Des Moines)	Any voter absent from the election precinct.	Apply in writing for official forms prior to election- Remit executed forms to appropriate official.
Kansas *	Anytime up to 20 days preceding an election	County election officer	Anyone absent from county of residence	Request official form from county election officer Remit the form properly sworn and notarized.

119

Registration Requirements (cont.)

State

Kentucky	Anytime except during the period 59 days before and 5 days after any primary or general election (10 days before any special election or city primary)	County Clerk (in Louisville, Board of Registration Commissioners)	No absentee registration
Louisiana	Consult local officials for place and dates of registration. Books close 30 days prior to any primary or general election.	Registrar of Voters of Parish of Residence.	No absentee registration
Maine	Times vary according to the population of the municipality. Consult your local official. Generally, a one week registration period is held one to two weeks prior to election.	Board of Registration or Board of Selectmen	No absentee registration
Maryland	Consult local officials for times and dates of registration. No one may be registered after the 5th Monday preceding or during the 10 days following a primary or special election (or after 5th Mon. preceding or during 15 days following a general election). Consult election board for additional registration periods.	Board of Elections	Absent civilian electors qualify under military voting provisions. Absentee registration is effected by casting an absentee ballot.

Registration Requirements (cont.)

Massachusetts	At times provided by local ordinance but not between 10 P.M. of the 31st day preceding and the day following a state election; between 10 P.M. of the 20th day preceding and the day following a municipal city election; or between 7 P.M. of the 29th day preceding and the day following an election for presidential electors.	City or Town Clerk	No absentee registration	
Michigan *	Anytime up to 5th Fri. before election. Registration effected after the 5th Fri. before election is valid for subsequent elections only.	City, Town or Village Clerk	Anyone who by reason of absence is unable to register in person.	Apply in writing to appropriate official for duplicate registration forms. Remit executed forms before the 5th Fri. before election.
Minnesota *	Anytime up to 20 days preceding an election.	Commissioner of Registration	Anyone absent from municipality or residence or because of religious discipline cannot appear in person.	Apply in writing up to 20 days prior to election for registration application form. Remit executed application to Commissioner of Registration.

Registration Requirements (cont.)

Mississippi *	Anytime up to 4 months prior to the general election (or 30 days before the primary). Check local registrar for times for precinct registration.	City or County Registrar	No absentee registration	Apply in writing to local official at least 30 days before primary or general election.
Missouri *	Books close in St. Louis County, no later than 5:00 P.M. of 24th day preceding any election nor sooner than 15 days after an election. In Jackson County and in cities of 300,000 - 700,000 on 4th Wed. prior to election. Check local officials for registration dates	Clerk of the County Court (in St. Louis and Kansas City, Clay, Jackson and St. Louis Counties, with the Board of Election Commissioners)	Electors absent from county of residence may register absentee only in counties under "local option" registration. (no absentee registration permitted in St. Louis County and in cities of 10,000 or more).	
Montana *	Anytime up to 30 days prior to a federal election (40 days prior to any other election).	County, City, or Town Clerk or Deputy Registrar	Anyone absent from County of residence.	Execute an official registration card before a notary public and remit to election official before close of registration. Residence and signature on application must be verified by two registered electors before application may be accepted.

122

Registration Requirements (cont.)

Nebraska	Anytime prior to 6 P.M. on the 2nd Fri. preceding an election	County Clerk (Election Commissioner in Douglas and Lancaster counties).	Any elector absent from his county of residence	Fill out information on the registration forms accompanying your absent Voter's Ballot. Have the forms notarized. Remit with the ballot.
Nevada *	Up to 9 P.M. of the 7th Sat. preceding any primary election (9 P.M. of the 6th Sat. preceding any general election).	County Clerk or Board of Registrars	No absentee registration	
New Hampshire	The Board of Supervisors of the check-list compiles and publishes the voter list. Any additions or corrections may be made at Board sessions but cannot be made after the "closing date", usually 10 days prior to election. Consult your local officials.	Board of Supervisors of the check-list	Any temporarily absent elector	Apply to Sect'y of State for an absentee registration affidavit not later than 45 days before election.
New Jersey *	Anytime, but no sooner than 40 days prior to election. If you apply 0-39 days prior to election, you will be registered for subsequent elections only.	County Clerk Commissioner of Registration or City Clerk	No absentee registration	

123

Registration Requirements (cont.)

		County Clerk	Any temporarily absent elector	Request affidavit of registration forms. Remit prior to close of registration.
New Mexico *	Anytime up to 5 P.M. of the 42nd day preceding election. Books reopen the Mon. following election			
New York *	Registration times and dates vary depending on location. Consult your local officials. In New York City, apply anytime except 10 days prior and 5 days after a primary. For the general election, Central Registration closes 30 days before and opens 30 days after, the general election. Precinct registration may also be held.	Board of Elections	Any voter (where personal registration not required); any voter absent and because of duties of occupation or business (where personal registration is required).	Request absentee registration form from Board of Elections. Remit and receive "enrollment blank". complete and return not later than 5 P.M. of the Fri. before election day.
North Carolina	Anytime up to 21 days before a primary or general election. Applications made within 21 days prior to an election are valid for subsequent elections only.	County Registrar	No absentee registration (but electors expecting to be absent during registration may apply in person anytime other than the usual registration period).	
North Dakota	No registration required			

124

Registration Requirements (cont.)

Ohio *	Consult local officials for time of the first general registration period. After the first general registration period, apply anytime up to 9 P.M., of 41st day preceding a primary or general election (up to 4 P.M. of 11th day preceding a special election) but no earlier than 10 days following an election.	Board of Elections	No absentee registration (But electors expecting to be absent during registration period may register anytime before a clerk at the office of the Board of Elections)
Oklahoma	Anytime up to 10 days prior to election. (Or register with the precinct registrar from 30th to 10th day before an election)	Sec'ty of County Election Board	No absentee registration
Oregon *	Anytime except within 30 days preceding the election.	County Clerk	If absent from county of residence but within the state, register at Office of County of temporary residence. If absent from the State, register by mail.	Request official registration card (postmark must be no later than 30 days before election) Remit executed card to County Clerk.

Registration Requirements (cont.)

Pennsylvania*	Generally, anytime except the period from 50 days prior to 30 days after each general and municipal election (50 days prior to 5 days after a primary election). Consult local officials.	Registration Commission	No absentee registration
Rhode Island*	Anytime up to 60 days preceding election.	Board of Canvassers and Registration	No general absentee registration (only shut-ins and Peace Corps members)
South Carolina	Persons registered before Jan. 1, 1898 are registered for life. Register up to 30 days prior to election. Re-register every 10 years.	Board of Registration	No absentee registration
South Dakota *	Anytime up to 15 days next preceding an election.	County or City Auditor or Town Clerk	Anyone absent from voting precinct or residence.	Apply to County Auditor for "Registration Application Form." Remit before close of registration.

Registration Requirements (cont.)

Tennessee *	Anytime up to 30 days before a primary or general election. Supplemental registration sessions may be held. Consult local officials.	County Election Commission	Any elector required to be absent from residence because of regular business or occupation.	Request registration forms from County Election Commission, County Courthouse. Remit executed forms in time to be received no later than 30 days before election.
Texas	Up to 31 days prior to an election.	Office of the County Tax Assessor-Collector (Registrar)	Any qualified elector	Request application form from County Tax Collector. Remit form not later than 31st day prior to election
Utah *	Anytime up to 10 days preceding election. Registration agents also hold registration sessions. Consult local officials.	County Clerk	Any temporarily absent elector	Request official forms from County Clerk. Remit to County Clerk.
Vermont	A checklist of voters will be posted 30 days before election. A meeting is held for the purpose of revising the checklist which, in any event, cannot be altered after 12 noon of the Sat. preceding a Tues. election.	Town or City Clerk or Board of Civil Authority	Any absent person.	Write to town or city Clerk requesting necessary forms Remit prior to the checklist deadline.

Registration Requirements (cont.)

Virginia *	On the "regular registration day" 30 days prior to election. Additional days will also be held. Consult local registrar.	County or City Registrar	No absentee registration
Washington *	Anytime, but at least 30 days before election	City Clerk or County Auditor	No general absentee registration, but persons temporarily residing outside of their county of residence, but within the State of Washington, may effect registration in their county of temporary residence.
West Virginia	Anytime up to 29 days prior to an election. You may register during that 29 day period for subsequent elections only.	Clerk of the County Court	Anyone absent from county of residence because of occupation or other necessary cause.	Request an "Application for Absentee Registration". Remit executed form no later than 30 days before an election.
Wisconsin *	Anytime up to 5 P.M. on the 3rd Wed. preceding election in cities with 200,000 population or more (up to 5 P.M. on the 2nd Wed. preceding election in other municipalities).	Clerk of the Municipality (Office of the City Board of Election Commissioners in 1st class cities).	Qualified electors temporarily located more than 50 miles from their legal residence.	Request "Affidavit of Registration" form. Remit prior to end of registration period.

128

Registration Requirements (cont.)

| Wyoming | Anytime up to 30 days before election. | Registry Agent or County Clerk, or City or Town Clerk. | Any absent elector | Apply to Appropriate official for the necessary "Oath of Applicant to Register." Remit executed form in time to be received no later than 15 days before election. |

+ Only provisions dealing with general civilian absentee registration are noted. Special rules and procedures often exist for ill or disabled voters. Consult your local registrar for details.

* Precinct registration may also be held. Consult local officials for dates and places.

APPENDIX II

Registration and Voting Information for Military Personnel

The state voting information shown on the accompanying chart is only applicable to members of the Armed Forces on active duty. All dates refer to the General Election on 7 November 1972.

State	Registration requirement for military personnel	To register while absent, send a completed FPCA to:	To request an absentee ballot, send a completed FPCA to:	
			Where	When
Ala.	Must register before absentee ballot can be sent.	Board of Registrars, county of residence. See Note 1 (27 October).	County Register, county of residence.	Between 23 Sep and 2 Nov.
Alaska	Must register before absentee ballot can be sent.	Lt. Governor, Pouch AA, Juneau, Alaska 99801. See Note 1 (8 October).	Same address as registration.	Between 7 May and 3 Nov.
Ariz.	State registration form sent with absentee ballot.		County Recorder, county of residence.	Between 5 Oct and 4 Nov.
Ark.	Registration is waived.		County Clerk, county of residence.	After 8 Sep.
Calif.	State registration form sent with absentee ballot.		County Clerk, county of residence.	Preferably before 8 Sep.
Colo.	Registered when FPCA for absentee ballot is accepted.		County Clerk, county of residence. (Denver: Election Commission). See Note 1(6 October).	Between 9 Aug and 3 Nov.
Conn.	State registration form sent with absentee ballot.		Town Clerk, town of residence.	At any time.
D. C.	Registered when FPCA for absentee ballot is accepted.		Board of Elections, District Building, Washington, D. C. 20004.	Before 31 Oct.
Del.	State registration form sent with absentee ballot.		Department of Elections, county of residence. See Note 1 (28 October).	At any time.
Fla.	State registration form sent with absentee ballot.		Supervisor of Registration, county of residence. See Note 1 (8 October).	After 23 Sep.
Ga.	State registration form sent with absentee ballot.		Board of Registrars, county of residence. See Note 1 (18 September).	Between 9 Aug and 2 Nov.

Hawaii	Registered when FPCA for absentee ballot is accepted.		County Clerk, county of residence.	Between 8 Sep and 28 Oct.
Idaho	Uses executed affidavit on ballot-return envelope.		County Clerk, county of residence.	After 8 Sep.
Ill.	Registration is waived.		Board of Election Commissioners or County Clerk, county of residence.	After 30 July.
Ind.	Registered when FPCA for absentee ballot is accepted.		Clerk of the Circuit Court, county of residence.	Between 8 Oct and 4 Nov.
Iowa	Uses executed affidavit on ballot-return envelope.		County Auditor, county of residence, or City or Town Clerk.	After 9 Aug.
Kans.	Registration is waived.		Secretary of State, Topeka, Kansas 66612.	After 3 Sep.
Ky.	State registration form sent with absentee ballot.		County Clerk, county of residence. See Note 1 (18 October).	Before 18 Oct.
La.	Must register before absentee ballot can be sent.	Registrar of Voters, parish of residence. See Note 1 (8 October).	Clerk of District Court, parish of residence. (Orleans parish: Civil Sheriff).	Between 8 Sep and 31 Oct.
Maine	Must register before absentee ballot can be sent.	Board of Registration or Registrar of Voters, municipality of residence.	Secretary of State, or City or Town Clerk.	At any time.
Mass.	Registered when FPCA for absentee ballot is accepted.		City or Town Clerk, place of residence.	At any time.
Md.	Uses executed affidavit on ballot-return envelope.		Board of Supervisors of Elections, county of residence or City of Baltimore.	Before 31 Oct.
Mich.	State registration form sent with absentee ballot.		City or Township Clerk, place of residence.	Between 24 Aug and 4 Nov.
Minn.	Registered when FPCA for absentee ballot is accepted.		County Auditor, county of residence.	At any time.

State	Registration requirement for military personnel	To register while absent, send a completed FPCA to:	To request an absentee ballot, send a completed FPCA to: Where	When
Miss.	State registration form sent with absentee ballot.		City or County Registrar, place of residence. See Note 1 (1 July).	After 8 Oct.
Mo.	Registration is waived.		Clerk of County Court, or Board of Election Commissioners, place of residence.	At any time.
Mont.	Registered when FPCA for absentee ballot is accepted.		County, City or Town Clerk, place of residence. See Notes 1 (8 October).	After 23 Sep.
N. C.	Registered when FPCA for absentee ballot is accepted.		Chairman, County Board of Elections, county of residence.	At any time.
N. Dak.	Registration is waived.		County Auditor, county of residence.	After 8 Oct.
Nebr.	State registration form sent with absentee ballot.		County Clerk, county of residence. (Douglas, Lancaster, Sarpy: Election Commission).	Between 9 Aug. and 3 Nov.
Nev.	Must register before absentee ballot can be sent.	Same address as registration.		Before 5 p.m. on 31 Oct.
N. H.	Registered when FPCA for absentee ballot is accepted.	Board of Registrars or Court Clerk, county of residence. See Note 1 (8 October).	Secretary of State, Concord, New Hampshire 03301.	At any time.
N. J.	Registration is waived.		County Clerk, county of residence.	At any time.
N. Mex.	Registered when FPCA for absentee ballot is accepted.		County Clerk, county of residence.	Before 28 Oct. (Overseas 10 Oct)
N. Y.	Registered when FPCA for absentee ballot is accepted.		Div. for Serviceman's Voting, 162 Washington Avenue, Albany, New York 12225.	Before 28 Oct.
Ohio	Registration is waived.		Clerk, County Board of Elections, county of residence.	Before noon on 4 Nov.
Okla.	Registration is waived.		Secretary, County Election Board, county of residence.	At any time.

132

Oreg.	Uses executed affidavit on ballot-return envelope.	County Clerk, county of residence.	At any time.
Pa.	State registration form sent with absentee ballot.	County Board of Elections, county of residence.	At any time.
P. R.	Must register before absentee ballot can be sent.	General Supervisor of Elections, San Juan, P. R. 00903. See Note 1 (21 February).	Before 1 Sep.
R. I.	Registration is waived.	Same address as registration.	Before 5 p.m. on 17 Oct.
S. C.	State registration form sent with absentee ballot.	Board of Canvassers and Registration, place of residence.	At any time.
S. Dak.	Registered when FPCA for absentee ballot is accepted.	Board of Registration, county of residence. See Note 1 (8 October).	At any time.
Tenn.	Registered when FPCA for absentee ballot is accepted.	County/City Auditor or Town/Township Clerk. See Note 1 (23 October).	Between 9 Aug and 28 Oct.
Tex.	Registered when FPCA for absentee ballot is accepted.	Election Commission, county of residence.	Preferably before 23 Sep.
Utah	Uses executed affidavit on ballot-return envelope.	Office of County Clerk, county of residence.	Between 8 Oct and 2 Nov.
Va.	State registration form sent with absentee ballot.	County Clerk, county of residence.	Between 28 Sep and 2 Nov.
Vt.	Uses executed affidavit on ballot-return envelope.	General Registrar, place of residence.	At any time.
Wash.	Uses executed affidavit on ballot-return envelope.	Town Clerk, place of residence.	After 1 July.
Wis.	Registration is waived.	Secretary of State, Olympia, Washington 98501.	At any time.
W. Va.	State registration form sent with absentee ballot.	City/Town Clerk, place of residence. (Milwaukee: Board of Election Commissioners).	After 8 Sep.
Wyo.	Uses executed affidavit on ballot-return envelope.	Clerk of County Court, county of residence. See Notes 1,2 (8 October).	Before 23 Oct.
		County Clerk, county of residence.	

Note 1: If you are not registered, you should complete the state's registration procedure in time to be registered by the date shown in parentheses.

Note 2: If you are not registered, you should include on your FPCA the notation "Registration application requested".

133

STATE	CIVILIAN REQUEST FOR ABSENTEE BALLOT	SOURCE OF ABSENTEE BALLOT	TIME WHEN VOTED BALLOT MUST BE RECEIVED BY ELECTION OFFICIALS
Ala.	In person 20 - 5 days prior to election	County Register	No later than day of election
Alaska	In person 15-1 day prior to primary or general election; by mail 6 mos. to 4 days prior to an election	District Magistrate, Deputy Magistrate of Election District or Lt. Governor, Pouch AA Juneau 99801	Postmark must be no later than day of election
Ariz.	Return executed "Application for Absent or Disabled Voter's Ballot" form within 30 days preceding Sat. before election	County Recorder	No later than 6 P.M. on day of election
Ark.	In person 15-1 day before election; by mail "Application for Ballot" form no sooner than 90 days before an election. Remit no sooner than 15 days prior to election	County Clerk	No later than 7:30 P.M. on Election Day
Cal.	Recommend at least 60 days prior to election	County Clerk (Registrar of Voters if a resident of Los Angeles, San Francisco, or Santa Clara Counties)	No later than 5 P.M. on day before election

Colo.	Written request must be received no earlier than 90 days before and no later than close of business on Friday immediately preceding primary or general election	County Clerk (Election Commissioner if a resident of Denver)	No later than 5 P.M. on day of election
Conn.	Not sooner than 45 days before election	Clerk of Municipality (Town Clerk for town and state elections; City Clerk for city election; Borough Clerk for borough elections).	No later than 6 P.M. of day before election. If election falls on Monday, no later than 12 noon on day of election.
Del.	Submit required form no later than 30 days before election. Request absentee ballot no later than 12 noon of day prior to election	Department of Elections	Before 12 noon on day before election
Dist. of Columbia	In person or by mail 15-7 days prior to election. Voter may cast absentee ballot in person during this period or may remit executed ballot by mail.	Board of Elections	By 8 p.m. on day of election.
Fla.	Anytime between 45 days and 5 P.M. of day before election	Supervisor of Registration	No later than 7 P.M. on day of election
Ga.	Not more than 90 days prior to election	Board of Registrars	No later than closing of the polls (7 P.M.) on Election Day
Hawaii	Not more than 60 days nor less than 5 days (10 days if applicant is outside the state) before election	County Clerk (City Clerk if resident of Honolulu)	No later than close of business on day before a primary election, nor later than 12 noon on 6th day following a general election

Ky.	"Application for Absentee Voter's Ballot." Remit the form postmarked no less than 20 days before election	County Court Clerk	Before closing of polls on Election Day
La.	Mail request from 60-7 days before election. In person between 19-6 days prior to election	Clerk of the District Court, Parish of Residence (Civil Sheriff in Parish of Orleans)	In time to allow delivery of ballot to Commissioner of Election on Election Day
Maine	By letter anytime before election	Clerk of city or town of residence (if with military, apply to Clerk or Sect'y of State)	Before 3 P.M. on day of election
Md.	Not later than 7 days before election	Board of Supervisors of Elections	No later than close of polls on Election Day
Mass.	Obtain an application form for an absent voting ballot. Remit before noon on day preceding election	City or Town Clerk	No later than close of polls on Election Day
Mich.	Request "Application for Absent Voter's Ballot" as early as 75 days before election, but no later than 2 P.M. of Saturday before election	City or Township Clerk (Village Clerk for village elections)	Before closing of polls on Election Day

Idaho	Between 60 days and 5 P.M. of the day preceding election	County Clerk	By 5 P.M. on day prior to election
Ill.	An "Affidavit and Application for Ballot" at least 60 days before election. Remit completed application between 30-5 days before election (or 30 days if in person)	Board of Election	No later than day of election
Ind.	Not more than 60 days prior to a general election; not more than 30 days prior to a primary election nor later than Saturday next prior to election	County Election Board (if with military, apply to Clerk of the Circuit Court)	No later than 6 P.M. on day before election
Iowa	Apply for application form any day not a Sunday, election day or holiday, not more than 40 days prior to election Submit to County Auditor.	County Auditor or City or Town Clerk	In time to be delivered to election officials before Election Day
Kansas	Between April 1st and the last Thursday preceding the August primary election, and between Sept. 1st and the last Thursday preceding the general election.	County Election Officer	By 12 noon on Monday preceding election (in counties where voting machines are used, ballots will be received until close of polls

Minn.	"Application for Ballot", remit form 45-1 days prior to election	County Auditor	Before closing of polls on Election Day
Miss.	In person between 10 and 2 days prior to election	Circuit Clerk of County (if with military, apply to City or County Registrar)	In time to be delivered to election officials no later than day on which returns of election are received and canvassed
Mo.	Official form, no earlier than 30 days before election. Remit executed form in time to be received between 30 and 4 days before and election (or, if application made in person, by 4 P.M. on day before election)	County Clerk or Board of Election Commissioners	No later than 4 P.M. on day before election (no later than closing of polls for ballots for President and Vice-President)
Mon.	Anytime between 45 days and 12 noon on day next preceding the election	County, City or Town Clerk	In time to be delivered to election officials before closing of polls on Election Day
Neb.	By letter as early as 90 days before election, but not less than "two clear days" prior to election	County Clerk (residents of Douglas, Lancaster and Sarpy Counties to the County Election Commissioner)	No later than 10 A.M. on the first Thursday following Election Day. Postmark must be no later than 12 midnight of day preceding election
Nev.	Anytime before 5 P.M. on Tuesday preceding election	County Clerk or Registrar	Before polls close on Election Day

N.H.	At anytime request an "Application for Official State Absentee Ballot", remit to Clerk	City or Town Clerk (if with military, apply to Sect'y of State)	In time to be transmitted to election officials before the closing of the polls on Election Day
N.J.	In writing for a "Civilian Absentee Ballot" at any time but no later than 8 days before election	County Clerk (state and county elections) Clerk of Municipality (municipal elections) (if with military, may also apply to Sect'y of State)	Before closing of polls on Election Day
N.Mex.	At least 10 days prior to election	County Clerk	In time to insure delivery to polling place no later than 7 P.M. on day of election
N.Y.	By mail for an "Application for and Absentee Voter's Ballot". Remit between 30th and 7th day before election	Board of Elections, county of residence (military apply to Sect'y of State)	No later than noon on day before election
N.C.	"Application for Absentee Voter's Ballot" not more than 45 days nor less than 6 P.M. on Wednesday before election. Remit no earlier than 45 days prior to election	Chairman, County Board of Elections (if with military, may also apply to Sect'y of State)	No later than noon of the Saturday just preceding election
N.Dak.	"Application for an Absentee Voter's Ballot". Remit within 30 day period before the election	County Auditor	Before polls close on Election Day (military voters, no later than one week after day of election)

Ohio	"Application for Absent Voter's Ballot". Remit no earlier then 30 days before election (60 days if outside U.S. Continental limits) nor later than 4 P.M. of 5th day before election	Clerk of County Board of Elections	No later than 12 noon of 4th day prior to election (military voters no later than 12 noon on Election Day)
Okla.	In writing between 30 days and 5 P.M. of Friday before election	Sect'y of County Election Board	In time to be in hands of officials no later than 5 P.M. on Friday preceding a Tuesday election.
Ore.	Within 60 days preceding election but not later than 8 P.M. on Election Day	County Clerk or Sect'y of State	No later than closing of polls on Election Day
Pa.	50 days before primary or general election and not later than 5 P.M. of 1st Tuesday prior to Election Day	County Board of Elections	No later than 5 P.M. on 1st Friday preceding election
R.I.	"Application for Absentee Voter Ballot." Remit no later than 5 P.M. on 21st day before election	Board of Canvassers and Registration	No later than 9 P.M. on Election Day
S.C.	"Application of Transportation Worker for Absentee Ballot". Remit no earlier than 15 days prior to election nor later than noon, 3 days before election	County or City Auditor or Clerk of the Town or Township	Ballot must be marked earlier than 15 days prior to election and remitted before polls close on Election Day. (Military voters, must reach Superintendent of local Election Board before polls close on Election Day)

S.Dak.	By letter anytime after the official ballots have been delivered to election officials	County or City Auditor or Clerk of the town or township	Ballot must be marked earlier than 15 days prior to election and remitted before polls close on Election Day (military voters must reach local election officials before polls close on Election Day)
Tenn.	"Absentee Voting by Mail Application" not more than 40 nor less than 8 days before election; in person request and vote ballot at County Election Commission between 20-5 days before election	County Election Commission	Before 10 A.M. on Election Day
Tex.	Submit an Affidavit requesting an absentee ballot, stating the reason for your absence, at least 60 days prior to election. Remit between 20th and 4th day before election	County Clerk	No later than 1 P.M. on Election Day (postmarked no later than midnight of day preceding election)
Utah	"Application for Ballot". Remit no earlier than 30 days before election	County Clerk	Before noon on day of the official canvass following election

Vt.	Write letter to Town Clerk requesting ballot; as a general rule apply no later than 9 P.M. of the 4th day preceding election	Town Clerk	Before closing of polls on Election Day
Va.	"Application for Ballot" between 40 and 5 days before election	Registrar, place of residence	Before closing of polls on Election Day
Wash.	Not earlier than 45 days nor later than the day before election	County Auditor (if with military apply to Sect'y of State)	No later than 10 days after the state primary election (15 days after the state general election) Military voters' ballots must be voted no later than Election Day; civilian voters ballots must be postmarked no later than Election Day
W.Va.	In person or by mail 60 days before election. Applications must reach Clerk's office no later than Saturday preceding the day of a primary or general election, or 3rd day preceding a special election	Clerk of the Circuit Court	Before polls close on Election Day

State Absentee Voting Requirements (cont.)

Wis.	In writing no sooner than 1st of the month 3 mos. before election, nor after 5 P.M. on the Friday imme-diately preced-ing election. In person no sooner than 1st of the month 3 mos. before election, nor after 5 P.M. on the day preced-ing election	City, Town or Village Clerk (City Board of Election Com-missioners if resident of Milwaukee)	Before closing of polls on Election Day
Wyo.	No earlier than 40 days before election	County Clerk (City or Town Clerk in muni-cipal election)	At or before the opening of the polls on Election Day

All states permit request to be made by the Federal Post Card Application.

APPENDIX IV

Summary of Leading Supreme Court
Decisions Affecting Voting Rights

Introduction

When lawyers present cases before the United States Supreme Court, they do not primarily argue that a given law or course of conduct is "right" or "proper" or "desireable". The determining consideration is whether or not the statute or procedure is constitutional. Thus, the actual wording of the Constitution, as well as the intention of the founding fathers, is of paramount importance. Before reading the case summaries, the reader should review the text of Sections 1 and 5 of the 14th Amendment and all of the 15th Amendment to the Constitution. These represent the most prolific sources of constitutional litigation in the field of voting rights. The case summaries that follow are not intended to be a complete list. They are only the major decisions of constitutional law in this rapidly expanding area.

Amendment XIV

Section 1. All persons born or naturalized in the United States, and subject to the jurisdiction thereof, are citizens of the United States and of the State wherein they reside. No State shall make or enforce any law which shall abridge the privileges and immunities of citizens of the United States; nor shall any State deprive any person of life, liberty, or property, without due process of law; nor deny to any person within its jurisdiction the equal protection of the laws.

Section 5. The Congress shall have power to enforce, by appropriate legislation, the provisions of this article.

Amendment XV

Section 1. The right of citizens of the United States to vote shall not be denied or abridged by the United States or by any State on account of race, color, or previous condition of servitude.

Section 2. The Congress shall have power to enforce this article by appropriate legislation.

Lassiter v. Northampton County Board of Elections, 360 U.S. 45 (1959)

A state-imposed literacy test for voters, fair on its face and applied in a non-discriminatory manner, is not violative of the 14th Amendment's equal protection clause. Literacy "has some relation to standards designed to promote intelligent use of the ballot," and is "neutral" as regards race, creed, color and sex. Lassiter proved particularly disappointing to advocates of voting reform who had hoped that voting rights for blacks could be guaranteed by judicial decision. This case demonstrated the need for specific Congressional legislation, which finally culminated in the Voting Rights Act of 1965.

Louisiana v. United States, 380 U.S. 145 (1965)

Louisiana's "interpretation" test for voter registration which required a potential registrant to interpret a provision of the Federal or State Constitution violated the 14th and 15th Amendments. The Court noted, "This is not a test but a trap sufficient to stop even the most brilliant man on his way to the voting booth." Louisiana is one of a series of cases invalidating various tests or devices used by southern states to disfranchise the black voter.

South Carolina v. Katzenbach, 383 U.S. 301 (1966)

Sections 4(a)-(d), 5, 6(b), 7, 9, 13(a) and certain procedural portions of Section 14 of the Voting Rights Act of 1965 are within Congress' power to enact under Section 2 of the 15th Amendment and therefore constitutional. This decision affirmed the right of the federal government to authorize suspension of literacy tests and related devices in certain states and political subdivisions and held constitutional the controversial "automatic trigger" provision. The decision also validated appointment of federal registrars to register voters and the requirement of prior approval by the federal court or the Attorney General before any State or political subdivision in which the automatic trigger had taken effect could institute any new voting qualification or procedure.

Katzenbach v. Morgan, 384 U.S. 641 (1966)

Section 4(e) of the Voting Rights Act of 1965 was held constitutional. Section 4(e) provided that completion of six grades in a non-English speaking school accredited in the Commonwealth of Puerto Rico was conclusively presumptive of literacy for voting requirements purposes. Morgan is well known for its implication that Section 2 of the 15th Amendment permitted Congress to pass any legislation it deems "appropriate" to guarantee the vote to non-white citizens.

Gaston County v. United States, 395 U.S. 285 (1969)

This case arose on a petition to reinstate a literacy test automatically suspended by Section 4 of the Voting Rights Act of 1965. The court denied reinstatement implying that an admittedly impartial literacy test, instituted in a state which had previously maintained a segregated school system, violates the 14th Amendment's equal protection clause. Such a test may be fair on its face, but it may have the effect of discriminating against blacks due to their inferior educational opportunity.

Harper v. Virginia Board of Elections, 383 U.S. 663 (1966)

The imposition of a poll tax in state or local elections works an invidious discrimination based upon wealth and is therefore a violation of the 14th Amendment's equal protection clause. The Court definitively stated that a state violates "the Equal Protection Clause. . . whenever it makes the affluence of the voter or payment of any fee an electoral standard." Harper lent the coup de grace to the poll tax which two years earlier had been banned in federal elections by the 24th Amendment to the Constitution.

Kramer v. Union Free School District No. 15, 395 U.S. 621 (1969)

A New York statute which restricted the franchise in school board elections to residents who (1) owned or leased taxable real property within the district; or (2) were parents or had custody of children enrolled in the local public schools was invalid. The Court held that a state could not limit the franchise to otherwise qualified voters unless "the exclusions are necessary to promote a compelling state interest."

Cipriano v. City of Houma, 395 U.S. 701 (1969)

A Louisiana law limiting the vote to property taxpayers in elections called to approve the issuance of revenue bonds by a municipal utility was held unconstitutional. The Court stated:

the challenged statute contains a classification which excludes otherwise qualified voters who are as substantially affected and directly interested in the matter voted upon as are those who are permitted to vote.

Thus, the Court found that the Louisiana statute, like the New York law in Kramer, violated the equal protection clause of the 14th Amendment.

Phoenix v. Kolodziejski, 399 U.S. 204 (1970)

Arizona's law permitting only property owners to vote in elections held for approving the issuance of general obligation bonds was unconstitutional. This was a further move in striking down property ownership requirements as a precondition to voting. Noting that only 14 states had such a requirement, the Court rejected the argument that limiting the franchise in this manner was necessary to protect property owners from excessive property tax burdens. All voters, not just property taxpayers, said the Court, had an interest in the outcome of the election.

Oregon v. Mitchell, 400 U.S. 112 (1970)

Certain provisions of the Voting Rights Act Amendments of 1970 were valid. These provisions included the right of Congress to suspend the use of all voting tests and devices, to abolish durational residency requirements in Presidential elections, and to establish a minimum voting age of 18 in all federal elections. The Court invalidated that part of the law which established an 18-year-old voting age in state and local elections, noting that such a change could only be effected by a constitutional amendment. The result was the 26th Amendment to the Constitution, finally ratified on June 30, 1971.

Evans v. Cornman, 398 U.S. 419 (1970)

State residents who have a vital interest in electoral decisions cannot be denied the right to vote simply because they reside on a federal enclave. In Cornman, the appellees were
residents of the National Institute of Health enclave in the state
of Maryland. They not only lived within Maryland's geographical boundaries, but were treated as state residents for census
and congressional apportionment purposes as well. The Court
held that Maryland's determination that these individuals were
not citizens of the state for voting purposes violated their right
to equal protection of the laws. The implication of this case for
military voters residing on a military installation is clear. If
the state treats such individuals as residents of the state, and if
they have a vital interest in electoral decisions, such persons
cannot now be arbitrarily disqualified from voting for failure to
meet the state's definition of a "resident".

Dunn v. Blumstein, 40 United States Law Week 4269 (March 21,
1972), U.S. (1972)

Tennessee's durational residency requirement as a prerequisite to voting violated the equal protection clause of the 14th
Amendment as well as the constitutionally protected right of interstate travel. Tennessee required one year's residence in
the state and three months residence in the county before permitting a resident to vote. In striking down the requirement (and
thereby striking down all similar requirements among each of
the 50 states -- see Chapter 1), Justice Marshall, speaking for
the court, stated:
> Durational residence requirements completely bar from
> voting all residents not meeting the fixed durational stan-
> dards. By denying some citizens the right to vote, such
> laws deprive them of 'a fundamental political right. . .
> preservative of all rights.' (quoting Reynolds v. Sims)
The right to travel was also specifically recognized.
> In the present case, such laws force a person who wishes to
> travel and change residences to choose between travel and
> the basic right to vote.
The high court held that Tennessee's reasons for upholding the
requirement, protection against fraud and insuring knowledge-
able voters, did not demonstrate a "compelling state interest".
The Court left open the question of how long a durational resi-

dency requirement could be constitutionally imposed by a state, but did note that "30 days appears to be an ample period of time" for a state to guard against fraudulent practices.

Williams v. Rhodes, 393 U.S. 23 (1968)

Certain Ohio laws which mandated stiffer requirements for third parties seeking a position on the ballot than those required for the Republican and Democratic parties was held invalid. One of the laws provided, for example, that major parties may retain their positions on the ballot by obtaining 10% of the votes in the last gubernatorial election. Third parties, on the other hand, were required to obtain signatures totalling 15% of the gubernatorial vote by early February of a Presidential election year. By holding that the equal protection clause requires the state to show a "compelling interest" for "imposing such heavy burdens," the Court noted its concern with:

> the right of individuals to associate for the advancement of political beliefs, and the right of qualified voters, regardless of their political persuasion, to cast their votes effectively. Both of these rights, of course, rank among our most precious freedoms.

Jenness v. Fortson, 403 U.S. 431 (1971)

Certain Georgia laws defining minor political parties and candidates and establishing procedures for gaining access to the ballot was held constitutional. According to Georgia law, a "political party" is defined as any political organization whose candidates received at least 20% of the vote at the most recent gubernatorial or presidential election. Those polling less than 20% of the vote are designated "political bodies". A nominee of a political body or an independent candidate may not take part in a primary election and may appear on the ballot only by filing a nominating petition signed by at least 5% of the voters eligible to vote at the last election for the office the candidate is seeking. The petition must be circulated in 180 days. In upholding this scheme, Justice Stewart, speaking for the majority, noted that the Georgia laws, unlike the Ohio laws invalidated in Williams v. Rhodes, assured free access to the ballot for independent and third party candidates.

Bullock v. Carter, 40 United States Law Week 4211 (February 24, 1972),   U.S.   (1972).

Texas' statutory scheme requiring payment of fees for political candidates was an unconstitutional deprivation of equal protection of the laws. Texas law provided for the party committee to apportion the estimated cost of the primary among the several candidates according to its idea of what is "just and equitable." Through this assessment procedure, fees ranged as high as $8,900 per candidate. No other method was provided for gaining a place on the ballot. While recognizing that the state "has a legitimate interest in regulating the number of candidates on the ballot," the court noted that " [i] t is uncontested that the filing fees exclude legitimate as well as frivolous candidates." The Court concluded that:

> the State of Texas has erected a system which utilizes the criterion of ability to pay as a condition to being on the ballot, thus excluding some candidates otherwise qualified and denying an undetermined number of voters the opportunity to vote for candidates of their choice.

Gomillion v. Lightfoot, 364 U.S. 339 (1960)

Racially gerrymandered voting districts violate the 15th Amendment. The Tuskegee, Alabama city boundaries were redefined under a 1957 statute which altered "the shape of Tuskegee from a square to an uncouth twenty-eight sided figure." The result was the exclusion of virtually all of Tuskegee's voting Negroes from the city boundaries. The case is known not only for its racial discrimination content, but as a forerunner of the apportionment decisions. Gomillion was one of the few cases prior to Baker v. Carr which intimated that the states do not have unlimited control over their political subdivisions.

Baker v. Carr, 369 U.S. 186 (1962)

A Tennessee citizen's complaint that his state's failure to reapportion its legislative districts abridged his constitutional right to equal protection of the laws could be adjucated in the courts. In this landmark decision the Court pronounced the now-famous one-person, one-vote rule stating, in effect, that the Constitution guarantees every American an equally weighted vote in the election of legislative representatives.

Reynolds v. Sims, 377 U.S. 533 (1964)

The one-person, one-vote rule of Baker v. Carr requires both houses of a state's bicameral legislature to be apportioned on a population basis. The existence of the malapportioned United States Senate (two Senators from each state regardless of population) was the result of a peculiar political compromise and does not justify a similar structure on the state level.

Gray v. Sanders, 372 U.S. 368 (1963)

Although calling their decision "only a voting case", the Supreme Court effectively extended Baker v. Carr's one-person, one-vote rationale to primary elections. In Gray, the Supreme Court invalidated Georgia's "county-unit system" of counting votes in the Democratic Party primary. According to this system, "units" were assigned to various counties on the basis of population. This resulted in the vote of each citizen counting less as the population of his or her county increased. This, the Court noted, was a violation of equal protection. "Once the geographical unit for which a representative is to be chosen is designated," stated Justice Douglas, "all who participate in the election are to have an equal vote."

342.73
R379

85244